THE POWER OF
AGREEMENT

I0445320

Prayer Guide

Global Prayer Network

The Power of Agreement Global Prayer Network: Prayer Guide

Copyright © 2022 Artherrine Grimes Hoskins

All scriptures are referenced in the King James Version except when noted. A variety of Bible versions were chosen for clarification purposes. Although the Bible must never be mishandled by private interpretation, the author's insights can be obscured by failing to select the words that explain the points emphasized. We pray that each version examined adds an element of personal revelation to the reader. Each version used and its abbreviations are listed below in alphabetical order.

Scripture quotations marked (AMP) are taken from the Amplified Bible, Copyright © 2015 by The Lockman Foundation. Used by permission.

Scripture quotations marked (AMPCE) are taken from the Amplified Bible, Copyright © 1954, 1958, 1962, 1964, 1965, 1987 by The Lockman Foundation. Used by permission.

Scripture quotations marked (CEV) are from the Contemporary English Version Copyright © 1991, 1992, 1995 by American Bible Society. Used by Permission.

Scripture quotations marked (CJB) are taken from the Complete Jewish Bible by David H. Stern. Copyright © 1998. All rights reserved. Used by permission of Messianic Jewish Publishers, 6120 Day Long Lane, Clarksville, MD 21029. www.messianicjewish.net.

Scripture quotations marked (ESV) are taken from The ESV® Bible (The Holy Bible, English Standard Version®), copyright © 2001 by Crossway, a publishing ministry of Good News Publishers. Used by permission. All rights reserved.

Scripture quotations marked (NIV) are taken from the Holy Bible, New International Version®, NIV®. Copyright © 1973, 1978, 1984, 2011 by Biblica, Inc.™ Used by permission of Zondervan. All rights reserved worldwide. The "NIV" and "New International Version" are trademarks registered in the United States Patent and Trademark Office by Biblica, Inc.™

ISBN: 979-8-9857477-0-6 (Paperback)
ISBN: 979-8-9857477-2-0 (eBook)
Library of Congress Control Number: 2022905933

Edited by: Michelle Williamson
Cover and Interior Design by: Master Design Marketing, LLC

Fiesta Publishing
PO Box 44984
Phoenix, AZ 85064
www.fiestapublishing.com

First printing edition 2022
Printed in the United States of America.
10 9 8 7 6 5 4 3 2 1

"If My people who are called by My name will humble themselves, and pray and seek My face, and turn from their wicked ways, then I will hear from heaven, and will forgive their sin and heal their land."
— 2 Chronicles 7:14 NKJV

Dedication

This book is dedicated to my Heavenly Father, Jehovah God, who gave me the vision for my first published work. Thank You for stirring me and making it obvious to me that I should do this project, NOW! To my Savior and Lord Jesus Christ of Nazareth, who is my chief intercessor and High Priest (Heb. 10:10), thank You, Lord Jesus Christ. To God be the glory!

To the memory of my beloved parents, Arthur Lee and Francis Lowe Aiden Grimes, I love you and am grateful for your constant support. Thank you for teaching me God's wisdom, godly fear, and how to pray.

To my husband of forty-five years, Harvey Eugene Hoskins, you have truly been my friend, encourager, supporter, and a stabilizing force in my life. Thank you for being with me and for me.

Thank you for being so patient with me. You have always inspired me beyond what I thought I could do. Only our Heavenly Father Jehovah knows how I love and appreciate you. I am so grateful.

To my precious children: Kimberly and Damon Harlan, Kendall, and Anna Hoskins, thank you for your encouragement and inspiration.

To my motivators: my six grandchildren, Nia, Jayla, Nazyr, Keanna, Kamora, and Kendall Jr., thank you for your love and hugs.

To my siblings: Theresa, Alton, Nina B. Travis, and Terry, thank you for always supporting and believing in me.

To Mother Mary Mimms, thank you for teaching me to pray the Word of God and to remain faithful to God.

Thank you to all my extended family and friends for your love.

I am so grateful.

GPN's History

The Power of Agreement Global Prayer Network (GPN), which started as Greater Nashville Prayer Network, is now over thirty-two years old. As GPN's founder and leader, I called for the wise and praying women to come forth to pray for families, churches, and the Nashville community in 1987. In 1990, at Rev. Bob Stout's business office, we became the Greater Nashville Prayer Network.

We were greatly blessed by the teachings on prayer from the late Pastor Charles Blackmon and his wife, Pastor Linda Blackmon, and we continue to hear from her prophetic voice. In 2013, the organization became nationally known as Warriors across the United States and began to pray for the first African American President, Barack H. Obama. The ministry became global after traveling to Ghana with Pastors Chris and Gina Inkum, praying with others in Africa, Israel, China, Mexico, Jamaica, and the Bahamas.

Currently, we have about fifteen consistent phone lines. For ten years, we met monthly at the Historic First Community Church under the direction of Pastors Glen and Ella Clay. In accordance with the prophecy given by Dr. Sandy Powell of Powerhouse Ministries in 2007, the ministry began to multiply rapidly with women joining the Mother's Line to command and commit their day to the Most High God Jehovah in Jesus' name. They pray for children in their sphere of influence. Father God Jehovah is continuously opening doors and closing doors for His Glory!

The purpose of this ministry is to teach and impart effective praying. We have two groups of individuals involved: (1) those in training, and (2) those of mature levels. We are seeing signs, miracles, and wonders! Since Pastor Yvonne Johnson taught on the subject of angels during a Monday night Nation(s) Prayer Line, testimonies have tripled regarding our angels from Jehovah God. Just as Scripture tells us, "the meek [in the end] shall inherit the earth and shall delight themselves in the abundance of peace" (Ps. 37:11 AMPCE).

Inside are prayers compiled that were written by GPN leaders.
So Grateful,
Mother Artherrine Grimes Hoskins, Nashville, TN
February 2021

The Prayer Lines

Dial in #615.307.6988 (Unless otherwise noted.)

Monday
Mother's Prayer Line
 6:15 a.m.–7:00 a.m. CST
 7:15 a.m.–8:00 a.m. EST
 4:15 a.m.–5:00 a.m. PST
Israel Prayer Line
 7:30 a.m.–8:30 a.m. CST
 8:30 a.m.–9:30 a.m. EST
 5:30 a.m.–6:30 a.m. PST
State, President, Nation(s) Prayer Line
 7:30 p.m.–8:30 p.m. CST
 8:30 p.m.–9:30 p.m. EST
 5:30 p.m.–6:30 p.m. PST

Tuesday
Men's Watchmen Prayer Line
 7:00 a.m.–7:30 a.m. CST
 8:00 a.m.–8:30 a.m. EST
 5:00 a.m.–5:30 a.m. PST

Wednesday
Mother's Prayer Line
 6:15 a.m.–7:00 a.m. CST
 7:15 a.m.–8:00 a.m. EST
 4:15 a.m.–5:00 a.m. PST
Prayer & Fasting Line
 12:15 p.m.–1:15 p.m. CST
 1:15 p.m.–2:15 p.m. EST
 10:15 a.m.–11:15 a.m. PST

Thursday

Brides of Christ Prayer Line (1st, 3rd, and 5th Thursday of each month)
- 7:00 p.m.–8:00 p.m. CST
- 8:00 p.m.–9:00 p.m. EST
- 5:00 p.m.–6:00 p.m. PST

Children/Youth Lift Me Up (319.527.4787)
- 6:30 p.m.–7:00 p.m. CST
- 7:30 p.m.–8:00 p.m. EST
- 4:30 p.m.–5:00 p.m. PST

Friday

Mother's Prayer Line
- 6:15 a.m.–7:00 a.m. CST
- 7:15 a.m.–8:00 a.m. EST
- 4:15 a.m.–5:00 a.m. PST

Hope & Healing Prayer Line (1st, 3rd, and 5th Fridays of each month)
- 7:30 a.m.–8:30 a.m. CST
- 8:30 a.m.–9:30 a.m. EST
- 5:30 a.m.–6:30 a.m. PST

Widows Prayer Line (4th Friday of each month)
- 7:30 a.m.–8:30 a.m. CST
- 8:30 a.m.–9:30 a.m. EST
- 5:30 a.m.–6:30 a.m. PST

Saturday

Marriage Prayer Line (3rd and 4th Saturday of each month)
- 8:15 a.m.–9:15 a.m. CST
- 9:15 a.m.–10:15 a.m. EST
- 6:15 a.m.–7:15 a.m. PST

Sunday

Family Prayer Line (2nd Sunday of each month)
- 7:30 p.m.–8:30 p.m. CST
- 8:30 p.m.–9:30 p.m. EST
- 5:30 p.m.–6:30 p.m. PST

Push Prayer Line
Monday through Saturday (781.448.0427)
5:00 a.m.–6:00 a.m. CST
6:00 a.m.–7:00 a.m. EST
3:00 a.m.–4:00 a.m. PST

9–1–1 Emergency Prayer Line (private line)
Sunday through Saturday (Daily)
7:14 a.m.–8:00 a.m. CST
8:14 a.m.–9:00 a.m. EST
5:14 a.m.–6:00 a.m. PST

Submit prayer requests to:
https://www.powerofagreementprayer.org/

Table of Contents

What Prayer Is

Prayer to me and to those who have impacted my prayer journey is communicating with our Heavenly Father by speaking to Him, to God, then listening and receiving the earthly permission for heavenly intervention.

The Power of Agreement Global Prayer Network (GPN) Ministry is raising up prayer intercessors. Intercessory prayer is the act of praying to God on the behalf of others. Prayer involves repentance, confession, praise, worship, adoration, spiritual warfare, and thanksgiving. Spiritual warfare is the concept of fighting against the evil forces; spirits that intervene in human affairs in various ways.

The goal of prayer for GPN is to allow the Holy Spirit to move us beyond "low-end prayers" (for example, "Now I lay me down to sleep…."), up and into high-level intercession warfare prayers (for example, "Your Word states in Matthew 15:13, 'Every plant that my Heavenly Father has NOT planted will be pulled up by the roots'"), using the Word of God.

Jesus was empowered for rich kingdom ministry by resting in God's glory and grace while being positioned in love. We find this revealed in Luke chapter 5 verses 15 and 16, "But the news about Him was spreading even farther, and large crowds were gathering to hear Him and to be healed of their sicknesses. But Jesus Himself would often slip away to the wilderness and pray" (NASB). Intercessors, it is time to slip away and pray.

It is my prayer that intercessory prayer will become a reality in your life and in the lives of all those who partake thereof. The best intercession is informed and Spirit-led prayers. Therefore, allow this prayer guide to empower your intercession and aid you in assisting in the kingdom work by ushering in the kingdom of our God and His Son, our Savior and Lord, Jesus Christ.

In His Service,
Artherrine Grimes Hoskins
Founder and Overseer of The Power the Agreement
Global Prayer Network Ministry
Apostle, Evangelist, Intercessor, Prayer Warrior

"Now this is the confidence that we have in Him, that if we ask anything according to His will, He hears us. And if we know that He hears us, whatever we ask, we know that we have the petitions that we have asked of Him."
—1 John 5:14 –15 NKJV

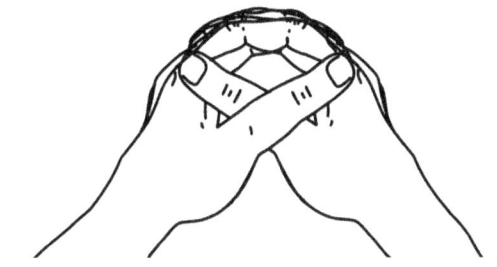

A Prayer of Worship and Praise unto the Lord Our God

Prayer Warrior Jacqui Rogers

Heavenly Father, Adonai, El Elyon, Elohim, El Olam, El Roi, El Shaddai, Immanuel, Almighty God, how majestic is Your name in all the earth. To the King of kings and the Lord of lords, You are the Alpha and the Omega, the beginning and the end, the first and the last, the one and only true and living God! You are full of all power. You are the Sovereign God of Abraham, Isaac, and Jacob, the Lord God of Israel.

We magnify Your holy name. We pray Your will to be done on earth as it is commanded in the heavens, and we thank You for Your many, countless blessings that You have bestowed upon those who love, hope, and believe in Your Son, Jesus the Christ! Emmanuel! God with us! Author and Finisher, Bread of Life, Bridegroom, Bright and Morning Star, the Chosen One, the Day Spring, the Deliverer, the Door, the Chief Cornerstone, the Kinsmen Redeemer, the Precious Lamb of God, Lion of the Tribe of Judah, Master, Messiah, Rabboni, the Truth and the Resurrection, Wonderful Counselor, Mighty God, Prince of Peace, Everlasting Father, for You and He are as One! And we are grateful for Your Holy Spirit who serves as Comforter and Teacher: We bow down and we bless You, Abba Father, for You are great and greatly to be praised! All the honor, all the praise, and all the glory belong to You, and we will not give it to another! Hallelujah!

In Jesus' name, Amen.

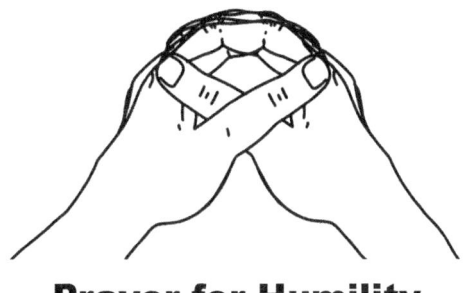

Prayer for Humility

Warrior Patricia A. Walker

Dear Heavenly Father,
I come to You as humble as I know how, trusting and believing that part of truly following You is humbling myself. Today, I choose to walk humbly with You, Lord, guided by Your Holy Spirit, following Your lead. Help me to hear You clearly and not to walk by pride or self-sufficiency. Lord, You humbled Yourself as a human to walk among us, so if I truly want to follow Your lead, humility must be a fundamental part of my walk. Thank You for helping me walk humbly with You and my brothers and sisters here on Earth. Help me be obedient to Your Word according to Micah 6:8, "The Lord has shown you, O mortal, what is good. And what does the Lord require of you? To act justly and to love mercy, and to walk humbly with your God."

Father, help me to not fall prey to my flesh and walk in arrogance or pride, but lift me up and cause me to live in harmony with others (Jas. 4:10). Help me to be sympathetic, to love as a sister (or brother), be compassionate and humble. Father, clothe me with humility toward others because You oppose the proud but give grace to the humble (1 Pet. 5:5).

Thank You, for Your grace and mercy that You make new to me each and every day.

Humility means casting all my cares upon You, Lord, for You care for me. It is recognizing that I am not almighty or invincible. Father God, I am nothing without You. I need Your guidance, and I need Your help. I want to gain honor in Your sight and not be too proud to ask for help from You or from others.

Help me humble myself so the lies of the enemy won't overtake me, and I count myself as equal with another. It is only then that I will stop attempting to be better than others and can love their hearts for the unique person You made them to be. Help me value everyone in this humble spirit so I may live a life worthy of You, Lord, pleasing You in every way, bearing fruit in every good work, and growing in the knowledge of God (Col. 1:10).

According to Matthew 23:12, "Whoever exalts himself will be humbled, and whoever humbles himself will be exalted" (ESV). Today, I renounce and break the curse of pride that came down my family bloodlines. I bind all boasting, selfish ambition, cursing, lying, anger, arguing and disputing, stubbornness, hardness of heart, unbelief and doubt, lack of wisdom and understanding, forgetfulness, lack of repentance and godly sorrow, backsliding, and departing from God.

And I loose the ministering spirits of God to restore any particle of my soul that has been removed, and to fill those vacancies with Godly character and attributes like holiness, purity, thankfulness, love, faith, hope, peace, compassion, and ultimately humility to resist the devil's temptations over me.

In Jesus' name, Amen.

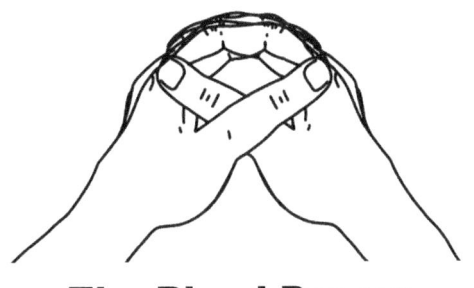

The Blood Prayer

The Global Prayer Network

D ear Heavenly Father,
We thank You for sending Your son, Jesus, to save us from our sins. We are reminded of how much You love us, for Your Word in John 3:16 states, "For God so loved the world, that he gave his only begotten Son, that whosoever believeth in him should not perish, but have everlasting life." Thank You, Jesus, for not coming down from the cross. Thank You for shedding Your blood so that we may live. Jesus, You are our source of life, thank You for Your blood that gives us victory over sin and death. The blood of Jesus protects, gives us strength. The blood is the source of our power; it heals and cleanses.

We plead the blood of Jesus and claim victory over every situation according to Your Word in Galatians 3:13. We plead the blood of Jesus over ourselves, over our bodies, minds, souls, and spirits; we plead the blood of Jesus over our spouses/relationships, children, grandchildren, spiritual children, extended family and friends, church, and ministries. We plead the blood of Jesus according to the Word in Exodus 12:13 which reminds us that there is protection through the blood. We cover our homes; let the blood of Jesus flow above our home(s), around and below it (them), we plead the blood of Jesus over our car(s), businesses, lands, and finances. We plead the blood of Jesus over the street where we live. We draw a line with the blood of Jesus around our dwellings so that no evil shall befall us nor shall any plague nor storms nor any evil entity come near us according to Psalm 91. We ask You, Lord, to send Your angels to guard us and our households and set a hedge of protection around us. We ask You, Lord, to break all plots of the enemy against us.

The blood of Jesus is life. Lord, let Your blood flow from the top of our heads to the soles of our feet. Blood of Jesus, heal us from everything that was not planted by You, and cleanse us from all impurities. The blood of Jesus has the power to heal according to Isaiah 53:3, which reminds us that by Your stripes we are healed. Blood of Jesus saturate our bodies, bones, organs, muscles, tissue, veins, arteries, every system; and replenish, restore, and renew. Blood of Jesus strengthen us. Satan, the blood of Jesus is against you, according to the Word of God in Revelation 12:11.

We are COVERED AND VICTORIOUS! REDEEMED BY THE BLOOD (Eph. 1:7)!

In Jesus' name, Amen.

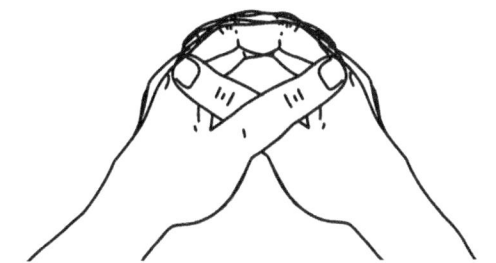

Prayer for Cleansing of the Heart

Mother Connie Martin

God my Father, Christ my redeemer, and Holy Spirit my companion, I thank You for being the Trinity. I come before You with a bowed down head, on my knees, and with an open heart to give You honor, praise, and glory. Thank You, Jesus, that I can be spiritually secure in Your love for me. God, You are the master weaver, and I thank You for Your blood that was shed for me, so I can worship You with a clean and pure heart. I know all that is good and perfect comes from You. I beseech You, God, and trust You to search my mind, my heart, and my spirit, and remove any uncleanliness. It is written that if we think it with our hearts so are we.

Cleanse my heart so that it is pure to do Your will on earth as it in heaven. When my heart is pure and clean, I can walk in the fruit of the Spirit. I can love my neighbors. I can forgive others as You have forgiven me. I can walk in love because You, God, are love. Please, God, if I sin let me repent so that my heart can stay clean and pure to serve You all the days of my life. It is written in Matthew 5:8, "Blessed are the pure in heart: for they shall see God." I want to have a clean heart and a righteous heart, so I can be with You in eternity. Open my eyes to see Your glory. Open my ears so I can hear from You. Open my heart so I can be more loving and draw closer to You so You will draw closer to me (Jas. 4:8).

I pray the Word as written in Romans 10:10, "For with the heart one believes and is justified, and with the mouth one confesses and is saved" and in 1 John 1:9, "If we confess our sins, he is faithful and just to forgive us our sins and to cleanse us from all unrighteousness" (ESV). Thank You, Jesus, for Your cleansing.

I am reminded of Your Word in Proverbs 4:23 which states, "Keep your heart with all vigilance, for from it flow the springs of life" (ESV). Cleanse my heart, God, of any unforgiveness in my spirit; remove anything that is not of You. I want to serve You in the newness of life that You give me each day, as You grant new grace and new mercy every day. There is victory in walking in Your path of righteousness.

Thank You, in the name of Jesus, for loving me beyond my understanding and thank You, God, for Your supernatural love for Your people. Spirit of the living God, fall fresh on me and renew my spirit to love and to serve You. Let me rejoice in Your love. Open my heart to only want and to do Your will. I know Your love is perfect. With my whole heart I seek You; let me not wander from Your commandments (Ps. 119:10 ESV).

I thank You, God, for loving me and for forgiving me of my sins and transgressions. I ask You, in accordance with Psalm 51:10 that You "create in me a clean heart, O God, and renew a right spirit within me" (ESV). Cleanse my heart and wash it white as snow, so that I can serve You in truth, spirit, commitment, and love. Cleanse my heart and spirit so I can be used by You.

In Jesus' name, Amen.

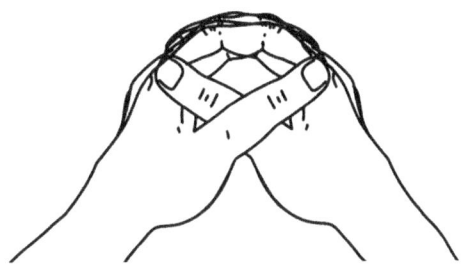

Forgiveness Prayer

Warrior Dr. Diana R. Williams

*For if you forgive other people when they sin against you,
your heavenly Father will also forgive you.* —Matthew 6:14 NIV

Dear Jehovah Shalom,
      You, Lord are peace and the lover of my soul! I praise Your holy name! You know everything about me, and when I am hurt, I run to You now for comfort and ask You to forgive everyone who has trespassed against me so that YOU can forgive me my trespasses. I pray for all who have wounded and offended me and place their names on the altar (list name[s]).

Please help me let go of all anger, bitterness, resentment, and unkindness in any form. It was not fair. It was not deserved. It was unexpected, and it did take a toll on me. But I make the choice today to absolve, let off the hook, pardon, release, and set (initials of person) free. Instead of continuing to be sad, disappointed, or angry about it, I thank You, Lord, that I have great peace in this situation. With Your help, I refuse to be hurt, vengeful, enraged, or made to stumble about (his/her/their) conduct any longer.

Help me be compassionate, loving, and merciful toward those who have offended me. From this moment on, I will walk in love with kind and patient behavior. I will not be rude, selfish, or quick-tempered. I am no longer stuck in rumination over wrongs that others do. Instead, I move forward in hope and conduct myself toward (him/her/them) in a manner that is pleasing to You. If at any time bad memories resurface to inflict pain or torment, I will cast my care upon You and pray this forgiveness prayer again. I can do all things—including forgiving others—through Christ. From this day forward, Your divine favor surrounds me as a protective shield, and I abide safely in Your arms where according to Isaiah 54:17, "No weapon formed against [me] shall prosper!"

In Jesus' name, Amen.

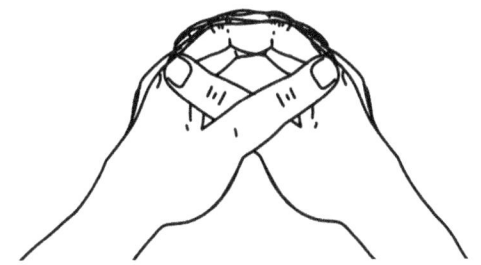

Psalm 23 Promise Prayer

Apostle Mother Eugenie Angela Mayers

The Lord Jesus Christ is my shepherd; I shall not want.
The Lord Jesus Christ makes me to lie down in green pastures.

The Lord Jesus Christ leads me beside the still waters.

The Lord Jesus Christ restores my soul.

The Lord Jesus Christ leads me in the paths of righteousness,
For the Lord Jesus Christ's name's sake.

Yea, though I walk through the valley of the shadow of death, I will fear no evil:
For the Lord Jesus Christ is with me.

The Lord Jesus Christ's rod and the Lord Jesus Christ's staff, they comfort me.

The Lord Jesus Christ prepares a table before me in the presence of my enemies;

The Lord Jesus Christ anoints my head with oil;

My cup runs over.

Surely goodness and mercy shall follow me all the days of my life;
And I will dwell in the house of the
Lord Jesus Christ Forever. (Adapted from KJV)
In Jesus' name, Amen.

Put On the Whole Armor of God

Apostle Mother Artherrine Grimes Hoskins

Good morning Heavenly Father! Good morning our Lord and Savior Jesus! Good morning our companion Holy Spirit!

We thank You for the victory for this day! We thank You for allowing us to arise to see another day of new mercies. We cover ourselves with the blood of Jesus and claim the protection of the blood for family, finances, home, business, ministry, spirit, soul, and body. We surrender ourselves completely in every area of our lives to You. We will not hate, envy, or show any type of bitterness toward our brothers, sisters, or our enemies, but we will love them with the love of God shed abroad in our hearts by the Holy Ghost. Pour Your love into our hearts, Holy Spirit. Pour Holy Spirit. Pour Holy Spirit. By faith, I (we) put on Your full armor right now.

By faith, I (we) put on Your belt of truth to cover our loins according to Psalm 51:6, "Behold, thou desirest truth in the inward parts: and in the hidden part thou shalt make me to know wisdom." May our lives be motivated by truth so we can maintain integrity. By faith, we put on the breastplate of righteousness to cover our hearts and chest cavities according to 2 Corinthians 6:7, "By the word of truth, by the power of God, by the armor of righteousness on the right hand and on the left." Thank You for the imputed righteousness of Jesus Christ. Help us understand that we are as righteous to You as Jesus Himself.

By faith, we put on the shoes of the gospel of peace to cover our feet according to Isaiah 52:7, "How beautiful upon the mountains are the feet of him that bringeth good tidings, that publisheth peace; that bringeth good tidings of good, that publisheth salvation; that saith unto Zion, Thy God reigneth!" Holy Spirit, help us to stand in Christ's victory this day. Help us be peacemakers and not troublemakers. Help us to bring Your peace to all we encounter today.

By faith, we take the shield of faith to cover our bodies defensively and offensively according to Hebrews 10:38, "Now the just shall live by faith: but if any man (or woman) draw back, my soul shall have no pleasure in him (her)" (emphasis mine). Remind us that Your protection completely surrounds us, even during Satan's most vicious attacks. May we trust You and Your Word today and not add fuel to any of Satan's darts. Thank You, Father, that we can go into this day without fear.

By faith, we put on the helmet of salvation so that we can stay sane and saved according to 1 Thessalonians 5:8, "But we belong to the day. So we must stay sober and let our faith and love be like a suit of armor. Our firm hope that we will be saved is our helmet" (CEV). Help us to live in the future tense. Make us clearly see that we belong to You through Christ's death and that Satan can never own us again.

By faith, we take the sword of the Spirit, which is Your Word according to Ephesians 6:17, "Let God's saving power be like a helmet, and for a sword use God's message that comes from the Spirit" (CEV). Thank You for the precious gift of Your Word; it is strong and powerful, the defensive weapon to defeat all evil. Help us to remember Your Word and use it today. Holy Spirit, help us to never forget that there is truth in the Word to defeat every lie Satan may ever tell us.

By faith, we add the last piece of armor, praying always with all prayer and supplication for all the saints according to Ephesians 6:18, "Praying always with all prayer and supplication in the Spirit, being watchful to this end with all perseverance and supplication for all the saints" (NKJV). Father, we ask You this day for a new and fresh anointing and to be covered in the blood of Jesus. Yesterday's anointing can't work for the task(s) for this new day. Anointing fall on us!

Now Heavenly Father, we praise and we thank You for the armor You have provided for us to dress in this day. Thank You, Father; we are completely covered now in the name of Jesus, in the blood of Jesus, and according to Your Word.

Father, we are Yours. Rise up big today within us, Father.

In Jesus' name, Amen.

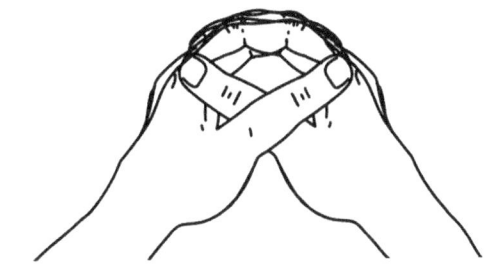

Warfare Prayer Points for Victory

Warrior Prophet Mark Korley

I call to resurrection every God-given dream and vision in my life that the devil tried to kill.

I command every demonic womb to open and release my blessings that it swallowed up.

I command a release of my body, soul, and spirit from every satanic chain.

I undress myself of every satanic garment of poverty, defeat, reproach, and failure.

I put off every filthy rag from my life.

I unclothe myself of the spirit of heaviness.

I clothe myself with the garment of praise.

I clothe myself with God's robe of righteousness.

I arm myself with God's armor of victory.

I invoke the supernatural, miracle-working power of God.

I call into action God's right hand of righteousness to heal, deliver, and save my life and everything born out of my loins.

I activate God's warrior angels to fight on my behalf.

O Lord God of war, arise and let thine enemies be scattered.

Oh commander of the Lord's army, arise in power and come to my rescue.

Let God's arrows of deliverance be released into my life and disperse all my enemies.

Let the fire of God descend from heaven and consume every unclean spirit opposing my destiny.

In Jesus' name, Amen.

Watchmen Prayer

Warrior Pastor Terrell Hunt

Father, I thank You for the divine assignment of a watchman, and I receive and obey such a call with gratitude and humility. As a watchman, I will cultivate my ability to hear the Holy Spirit and keep my heart pure, so I can properly discern the areas You have assigned. Lord, I desire to pray Your purposes and protection over Your people, geographical area, and/or nation.

I ask for dedication, focus, consistency, and perseverance as I discern and pray it into existence. I now ask You for insights and grace, so I can pray effectively with a watchman's spirit. Father, reveal the intimate needs of those for whom I should intercede. I will wait upon You, looking and listening to hear what You are saying. As a watchman on the wall, I will remain alert for any attempt of the enemy to attack or infiltrate my assigned area(s). I will not be unaware of the enemy's schemes to disrupt, destroy, or divide.

Lord, I will stand, watch, and station myself on the watchtower. I will keep watch to see what You will say to me as I ask, Lord, what are You doing in my life, church, home, family, or city this day. Is there something, Father, You are calling Your people to do in cooperation with You? Father, whatever I do as a watchman, no matter what it is, in word or deed, I will do everything in the name of the Lord Jesus and in dependence upon His love, power, and authority as I give worship and praise to Your name.

In Jesus' name, Amen.

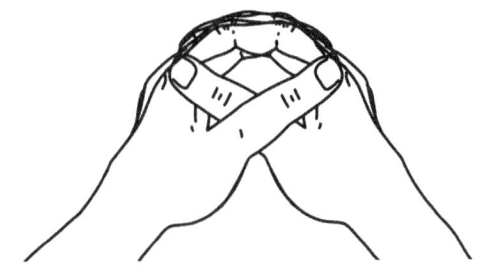

Commanding the Morning

Apostle, Evangelist, Intercessor and Prayer Warrior,
Founder and Overseer of Power of Agreement (GPN, Inc.)
Artherrine Grimes Hoskins

One can discover the secrets of doing exploits for God by specifically decreeing and declaring a thing and commanding our day. When you use this prayer method, there will be an improvement in the way you think, talk, live, pray, and believe. Commanding your morning can release overcoming power in your heart. You can take charge of your day by commanding your morning.

We can take control of our destinies by learning to command our mornings. Command means to order with authority, to take charge of, and to guard. God's Word says, "Set your words in order before me; take your stand" (Job 33:5 ESV). And Ephesians 6:14 and 18 tells us, "Stand your ground…. Stay alert and be persistent in your prayers" (NLT).

As a born-again believer in the Lord Jesus Christ, you have been commanded by God to have authority and power. You have been empowered by the Lord Jesus Christ to exercise authority over the sun, moon, the stars, and all the elements of heaven. God has put all things under your control (Ps. 8:6).

Our survival in the last days depends on deep warfare prayers. While on earth, Jesus spent time in prayer to establish God's divine agenda in the earthly realm. Jesus dislodged evil and downloaded victory, success, and prosperity in His day. He was exposing His disciples to the discipline of kingdom living.

To command means to keep watch, regulate, give orders to, instruct, dictate, exercise authority, decree, control, supervise. Let us ask Jesus like the disciples did in Luke 11:1 how to pray right now: *Lord Jesus, teach us how to pray Your type of prayers; teach us how to obtain results in prayer. Teach us how to command the morning and the day. Teach us how to speak so that the whole creation will listen and obey.*

The daily affirmations of Jesus in Luke 11 cannot work until we command them into action.

Many have died before their destinies are met; many have died before their time (premature deaths). Most of the problems encountered during our day could be averted if we would take the time to command our morning. The enemy knows how important the morning is. The reason the enemy introduces distractions into our lives is because he knows the importance of commanding our mornings.

Be mindful that the morning is the beginning of the day and of life. Therefore, learn to command your morning, and you will get what you speak.

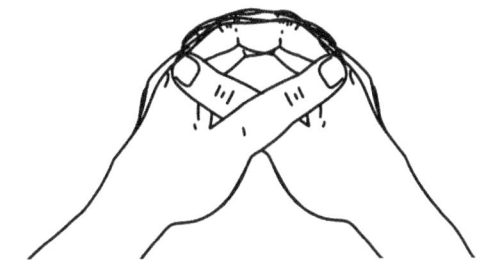

Prayer Points to Command Your Morning

Power of Agreement Global Prayer Network

By praying these prayer points, you can deprogram any evil programmed against you. Start by singing songs of praises and thanksgiving to God for giving you another new day! I encourage you to form the habit of prevailing in prayer over enemies daily.

I exercise the power given to me by the Lord, Jesus Christ and take authority over this day in the name of Jesus (Luke 9:1).

I confess that this is the day the Lord has made, I will rejoice and be glad in it (Ps. 118–24).

I speak unto you, sun, moon, and stars: you will not smite me this day, in the mighty name of Jesus (Ps. 121:6-8).

I command the morning to take control of the ends of the earth, in Jesus' name (Job 38:12).

I receive Your lovingkindness every morning (Ps. 143:8).

Lord, release the beauty of Your holiness from the womb of the morning, in the name of Jesus (Ps. 110:3).

Lord, teach my hands to war and my fingers to fight this day, in Jesus' name (Ps. 144:1).

Let all the enemies that make war with the lamb be destroyed, in the mighty name of Jesus (Rev. 17:14).

Deliver me from my strong enemy, from them that are too strong for me, Lord (Ps. 18:17).

Let Your light break forth in my life as the morning this day, in Jesus' name (Isa. 58:8).

Let Your judgments come upon the enemy morning by morning (Isa. 28:19).

Lord, You awaken me morning by morning; You awaken my ear to hear as the learned (Isa. 50:4).

I will not be afraid of the arrow that flies by day or the terror that comes by night (Ps. 91:5).

I bind, expose, and cast out any demon, in Jesus' name, that attempts to come undetected into my life (2 Sam. 19:3).

Lord, deliver me and bring me into a large place (Ps. 18:19).

I bind the operation of the screech owl night monster from operating against me, in the name of Jesus (Isa. 34:14).

I will not be afraid of the terror by night, and, in the name of Jesus, I rebuke every night bird that attempts to visit me at night (Ps. 91:5).

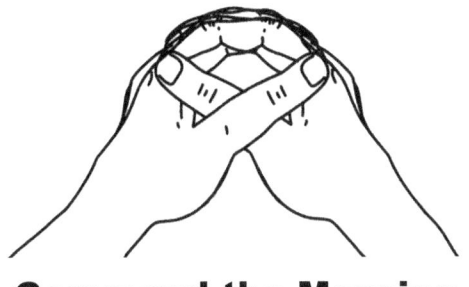

Command the Morning

Warrior Pastors Chris and Gina Inkum

Prayer 1 of 3

Every evil equation written in the cycle of the sun, moon, and stars against me, my family, and my loved ones, change in my (our) favor in the name of Jesus.

Illustration

If someone sets a thermostat to seventy degrees, the unit will continue to work based on that programmed equation unless someone changes the setting to seventy-five degrees. One plus one equals two (1+1=2); this is true no matter where you go on this Earth and regardless of the language. The only way the answer to any equation will change is if one of the variables in the equation changes. Unless you change a variable in an equation, your result will always be the same.

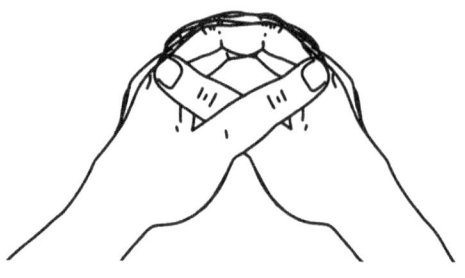

Command the Morning

Warrior Pastors Chris and Gina Inkum

Prayer 2 of 3

Lord, give me divine alertness to recognize divine opportunities in the mighty name of Jesus.

Explanation

Often, we are surrounded by many opportunities we do not recognize. It is a tragedy to suffer hunger in the midst of plenty because of the inability to recognize opportunities. This prayer will open doors that are not visible to others and cause a divine breakthrough in your life.

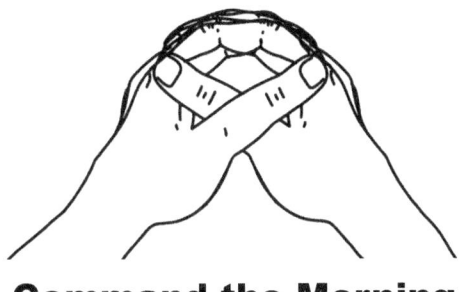

Command the Morning

Warrior Pastors Chris and Gina Inkum

Prayer 3 of 3

I take divine insurance and assurance against all forms of accidents and tragedy in the mighty name of Jesus. I decree and I declare that my loved ones and I will never ever become victims of circumstances. Our steps are ordered of God.

Explanation

This prayer will cause you to be at the right place, at the right time, with the right people doing the right thing. The insurance policy of God is the only insurance policy without a deductible or limit.

In Jesus' name, Amen.

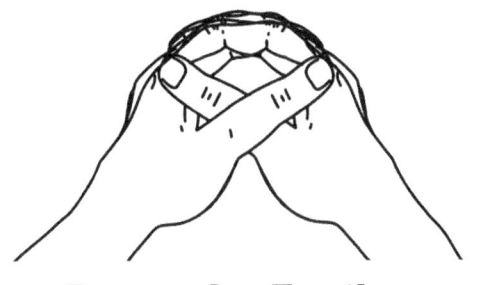

Prayer for Fasting

Warrior Minister Crystal Bouldin

Father, in the name of Jesus, as according to Your Word, I declare a fast not obvious to men, but only to You (Matt. 6:16–18). I seek Your face and revelation wisdom through Your supernatural power for my life, my family, my finances, my ministry, my business. I offer my body as a living sacrifice, holy and pleasing to You. Help me to grow to maturity, that my eyes will be enlightened to the hope of Your calling (Rom. 12:1–2).

Reveal unto me Your purpose and plan for my life. I desire to experience a deeper, more intimate relationship with You. To better focus in accomplishing and fulfilling Your perfect plan for my life. I pray as my body is cleansed by this fast, I am transformed by the renewing of my mind that I may prove what is the good, pleasing, and perfect will of God (Rom. 12:1–2).

In Jesus' name, Amen.

Prayer for Hope

Warrior Dr. Diana R. Williams

"For I know the plans I have for you," declares the LORD, "plans to prosper you and not to harm you, plans to give you hope and a future."
—Jeremiah 29:11 NIV

Dear Adonai, my great Lord,
Thank You, Elohim, the All-Powerful Creator for allowing each of us to come before You in prayer and praise! You are good! You are holy! You are faithful! We love You, Lord, with all of our hearts, with all of our souls, with all of our minds, and with all of our strength. Thank You for loving us so completely and lavishly. Your love is extravagant and perfect toward us, so we celebrate You today!

We thank You for this opportunity to come boldly to the throne of grace to utter this prayer of hope.

We know we must have hope if we want to live the blessed and abundant lives You have planned for us. Your Holy Word urges all who put their hope in the Lord to be strong and courageous. According to Psalm 71:5, You are our hope, O Lord God! No matter what happens in our lives, we must remain full of hope, as we recall that it is through Your mercies that we are not consumed. Your compassions fail not. Great is Your faithfulness!

According to Romans 5:3–5, "We…glory in tribulations, knowing that tribulation produces perseverance; and perseverance, character; and character, hope. Now hope does not disappoint, because the love of God has been poured out in our hearts by the Holy Spirit who was given to us" (NKJV).

31

So we thank You, Lord, for this hope. It is audacious hope, earnest hope, faithful hope, glorious hope, patient hope, resolute hope, tenacious hope, and transformative hope that anchors our soul. The Bible tells us in Romans 8:24–25, "For we were saved in this hope, but hope that is seen is not hope; for why does one still hope for what he sees? But if we hope for what we do not see, we eagerly wait for it with perseverance" (NKJV).

For those who have lost hope or have low hope, we ask that You restore their hope with renewed faith and confidence. Help them remember that You delivered in the past and made a way out of no way. You, Lord, turned what looked hopeless into something victorious so we can look toward the future with hope. This hope is active and moves us forward, even when we cannot see it. Therefore, please help us hold fast to the confession of our hope without wavering.

Help us remember that Your promises are sure! We declare, Dear Lord, that each plan You have for us will manifest, and we will thrive in triumph as hopeful people who have chosen to live victoriously. As we end this prayer, we thank You for the resurgence of hope, unrestrained joy, and the perfect peace that surrounds us at this very moment. It is in the mighty name of Jesus that we pray and declare it so. Amen.

"Now may the God of hope fill you with all joy and peace in believing, that you may abound in hope by the power of the Holy Spirit" (Rom. 15:13 NKJV).

In Jesus' name, Amen.

Prayer for Healing

Warrior Catherine Floyd

Jesus, You are the Word who created earth, all creation therein, and all mankind. Thank You, Father, for sending Your Word to heal us body, soul, and spirit. You are awesome in all Your ways. I bow down in Your presence, and I reach up and receive Your healing power.

We stand on Your Word. It will not return unto You empty. It will accomplish all that You want it to. It will succeed. It will prosper everywhere it is sent (Isa. 55:11). Father, send Your Word and heal (insert a name) according to Your will, Your great grace, and Your mercy.

Almighty God, Lord, Savior, and Healer, I praise You and bless You for the grace and mercy You give daily (Ps. 103). Thank You for Your unfailing love and powerful miraculous acts (Ps. 107:19–21). "Therefore God exalted him to the highest place and gave him the name that is above every name, that at the name of Jesus every knee should bow, in heaven and on earth and under the earth" (Phil. 2:9–10 NIV).

The name of Jesus is above the name of cancer, arthritis, diabetes, mental and emotional illnesses, and every other kind of illness, sickness, disease, and pain. All must bow to the name of Jesus. You heal the brokenhearted (Ps. 147:3). You heal all diseases (Ps. 103:2–4, Ex. 15:26, Isa. 53:4–5). You hear and answer the cry of the righteous for healing (Ps. 34:17–22; Ps. 6:2; Ps. 30:2).

You protect and keep Your righteous servant saints and restore them from illnesses (Ps. 41:2–3; Matt. 9:35). You shed Your blood for healing all that concerns us body, soul, and spirit (Isa. 53). Father God, because You sent Your Word and because of the shed blood of Jesus Christ, I ask You in the name of Jesus to heal (insert name). Let Your healing power flow through every internal organ, artery, vein, muscle, sinew, nerve, and bone from the top of the head to the soles of the feet.

In Jesus' name, Amen.

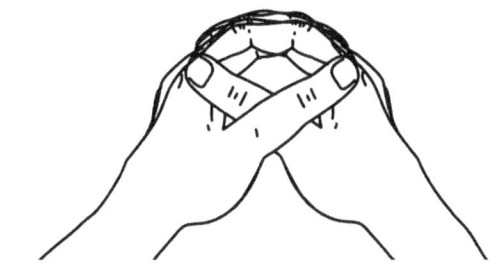

Prayer for Healing from Cancer

Warrior Gwelthalyn Huff

Heavenly Father,
I believe I became a cancer conqueror not because I went into remission, but because I constantly renewed myself and my lifestyle. Your Word states in Matthew 15:13, "Every plant, which my heavenly Father hath not planted, shall be rooted up."

Cancer was not planted by God. Your death at the cross pulled sickness and disease up from the roots. I don't fail to remember cancer is a spiritual journey, making me aware and appreciative of everything You have given me, and more grateful of every moment I have, more loving, kinder, and dedicated to making this place better in Jesus' name.

Thank You, God, for healing me.

In Jesus' name, Amen.

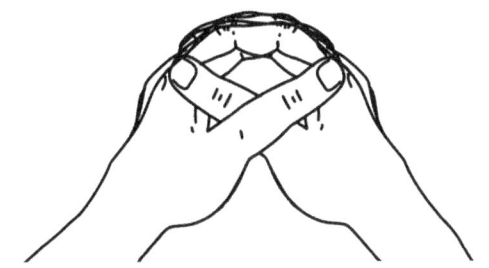

Prayer against Aggressive Diseases & Viruses

Warrior Tangela M. Jones Grimes

The following prayer was birthed from the Unite714 Covid prayer line. While praying for those battling Covid, we realized that other aggressive diseases, illnesses, and viruses were still lurking. We vowed to stand in the gap for all those who are battling aggressive diseases, illnesses, and viruses knowing, "And when he had called unto him his twelve disciples, he gave them power against unclean spirits, to cast them out, and to heal all manner of sickness and all manner of disease" (Matt. 10:1).

Dear Heavenly Father,

We come to You giving You the honor, the glory, and the praise for You are worthy of all praise. We praise You God for being who You are. You are a loving God, merciful God, caring God, omniscient God. Diseases and sickness are not foreign to You. Lord, You are the Great Physician, and Your power, knowledge, and abilities are without limitation. We praise You, Jehovah Rapha, our God who heals. It was You who raised Lazarus from the dead (John 11:38). You healed the woman with the issue of blood (Matt. 9:20–22). You made the lame to walk, and You restored sight (Matt: 11–5), You are worthy to be praised (Ps. 96:4). You are the same God yesterday, today, and forever more (Heb. 13:8). The things You did then, You can surely do now.

Forgive us, Lord, for our sins and help us forgive others, just as You have forgiven us. Unforgiveness is like poison in the bodies of Your people. It eats away at the flesh. Help us walk in forgiveness so we can live a healthy life. Forgive us, God, for the times we did not care for our bodies the way that we should. We reject anything that is not good for us including bad eating habits, contrary ways of thinking, and toxic foods and environments. Transform minds, change our way of thinking, redirect our footsteps. Help us live lives that are whole, healthy, and pleasing to You.

Thank You, God, for Your love. Thank You for Your many blessings. Thank You for bearing our burdens and for caring for us day-by-day. Thank You for being the lifter of our head when hopelessness and despair seem to take over and we want to give up. Help us trust You with every area of our lives, especially as it concerns our health.

Lord, You created all mankind. You created our bodies with many parts, each with a specific function. Our great maker, the giver of life, You know all about Your children, and we come to You, the ultimate healer, doctor, surgeon, physician, we cry out, "Help us, Lord!" Lord, heal our bodies so they can operate the way that You designed them.

We pray for all those who need a healing. Lord, heal (insert specific name(s)) so that their body can operate the way You designed it. We bind heart disease, strokes, aneurysms, blood clots and blockage, hemorrhage, diabetes, hypertension, kidney disease, liver disease, and all forms of cancer, Covid, flu, pneumonia, and every bold, aggressive, resistant disease, illness, and virus including those that seek to torment, cause labored breathing, unbearable pain, restricts movement and life, attempts to hinder one's praise, tries to steal joy, and seeks to destroy mentally, physically, and spiritually.

We loose healing in the name of Jesus, joy in the name of Jesus, a sound mind in the name of Jesus, strength in the name of Jesus, relief in the name of Jesus, peace in the name of Jesus, mobility in the name of Jesus, happiness in the name of Jesus, and life in the miraculous name of Jesus.

Father, break these diseases, illnesses, and viruses down. Strip them of their power. Slow down and completely destroy the rate in which they attack. Sever them from the core and restore to perfect health. We plead the blood of Jesus over their bodies. Your blood, Jesus, washes and cleanses from all impurities. Every disease, illness, and virus, GO in the name of Jesus!

We decree and declare that all are healed according to Exodus 23:25–26; sickness is far from them. Our loved ones and friends will not die a premature death. They shall live, and their number of days will be fulfilled. We decree and declare that they have strength, and their strength shall be renewed according to Isaiah 40:31, 41:10.

Lord, You took their infirmities and bore their sicknesses (Matt. 8:17); by Your stripes they are healed. Lord restore, renew, and rejuvenate. Give peace and joy in their hearts. Help them keep moving, stretch their faith, build up their trust, and strengthen their relationship with You.

Scripture says:

> Is anyone among you in trouble? Let them pray. Is anyone happy? Let them sing songs of praise. Is anyone among you sick? Let them call the elders of the church to pray over them and anoint them with oil in the name of the Lord. And the prayer offered in faith will make the sick person well; the Lord will raise them up. If they have sinned, they will be forgiven. Therefore, confess your sins to each other and pray for each other so that you may be healed. The prayer of a righteous person is powerful and effective. (James 5:14–16 NIV)

We claim healing and victory as we pray this prayer of faith. Help us be confident in Your power, the power of Your grace. Lord, we thank You for what You are doing. We trust You.

In Jesus' name, Amen.

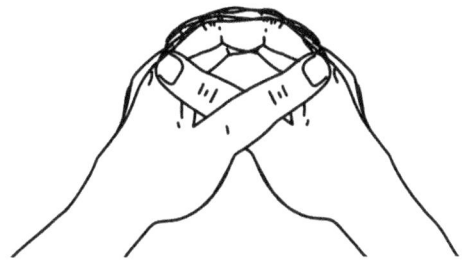

Decrees for Success

Power of Agreement Global Prayer Network

The Bible declares in Job 22:28, "Thou shalt also decree a thing, and it shall be established unto thee: and the light shall shine upon thy ways."

I declare that the peace of God will enter into my mind and destroy all confusion sent by the enemy according to Philippians 4:7.

I decree and declare that the joy of the Lord is my strength according to Nehemiah 8:10.

I declare that I will use wisdom when making decisions according to Proverbs 4:7.

I decree and declare that the plots of the enemy against me are canceled in the name of Jesus Christ according to John 10:10.

I decree that I am a blessing to the nation(s) according to Malachi 3:12.

I decree and declare that my children are purpose-filled by the Lord according to Matthew 21:16.

I decree that no weapon formed against me will prosper according to Isaiah 54:17.

I decree that the healing hand of God will cancel every sickness or disease and replace it with wholeness according to Isaiah 53:5.

I decree and declare that I am no longer a victim but a victor in Jesus' name according to 1 John 4:4.

I decree that I can do all things through Christ who strengthens me according to Philippians 4:13.

I decree and declare that the generational curses in my life are broken according to Matthew 11:29.

I decree and declare that I have the authority to bind every demon and ungodly spirit according to Matthew 16:19.

In Jesus' name, Amen.

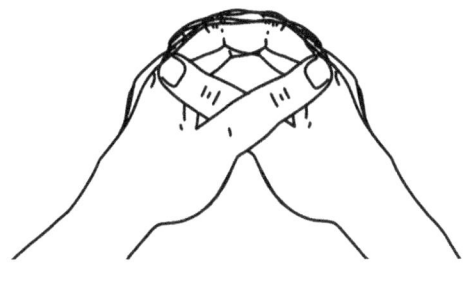

Prayer for Business

Warrior Husband Harvey E. Hoskins, CPA

The Bible says you shall be the head and not the tail, so say these prayers as you prepare to submit a business proposal to win profitable contracts. God will supply your needs. He promises to bless you and give you life more abundantly. When you understand God's mindset about riches, you will be amazed at the blessings that will overtake you.

I claim the contract in the mighty name of Jesus Christ.

Lord, hammer my matter into the mind of those who will assist me/us so that we do not suffer from demonic loss of memory.

I paralyze the handiwork of household enemies and envious agents in this matter in the name of the Lord Jesus Christ.

Let all adversaries of my breakthrough be put to shame by fire in the name of Jesus Christ.

I claim the power to overcome and excel among all competitors in the name of Jesus Christ.

Let the decision of the panel be favored unto me/us in the name of the Lord Jesus Christ.

Read Joshua 1:9 before you attend interviews and submit contracts. Joshua 1:9 states, "I have commanded you to be strong and brave. Don't ever be afraid or discouraged. I am the LORD your God and I will be there to help you wherever you go" (CEV). Praise the Lord Jesus Christ for answered prayer(s).

In Jesus' name, Amen.

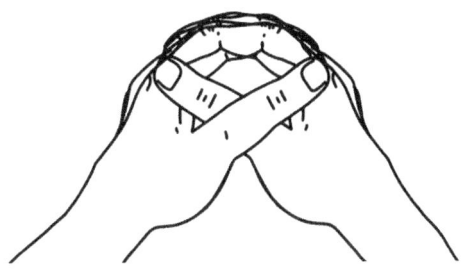

Prayer for Families

Warrior Pastor Deborah Holt-Foster

Our Lord, Our Mother, Our Father, Our Everything God, Before You, Lord, we come with heads bowed and some bodies bent with an expectation, Lord, that You will hear our prayer. Lord, we are struggling in this season. Lord, we are confused in this season. Lord, we are hurting in this season. Lord, we are spiritually divided in this season. Lord, we have misplaced our love, our unity, and our steadfastness in this season because many in our family do not have a relationship with You. When we don't have a relationship with You, Lord, it is often difficult to have a relationship with one another.

Lord, as a family we pray for love, respect, acceptance, and unity. As a family we plead the blood of Jesus over our family members who are scattered mentally, physically, emotionally, financially, and spiritually. We pray that in our mess, Lord, that we will unite without hostility; that we will unite without selfishness; that we will unite despite our differences; that we will unite in love.

Lord, we pray that You will help us forgive one another so we may live healthy fulfilling lives because unforgiveness creates physical illness.

Father, we pray that as we face each tomorrow that we would turn from our wicked ways and seek Your face. Lord, we pray that our family members who don't know You in the pardon of their sins will accept You into their hearts. Lord, we pray that each day continues to bring new mercies and new opportunities in You.

Keep us grounded. Keep us steadfast, unmovable, and always abounding in You.

In Jesus' name, Amen.

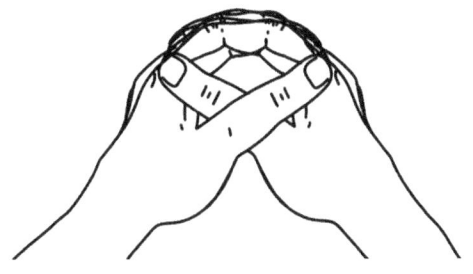

Peace in the Family

Mother Artherrine Hoskins

Father, in the name of Jesus, I thank You that You have poured Your Spirit upon our family from on high. Our wilderness has become a fruitful field, and we value our fruitful field as a forest. Justice dwells in our wilderness and righteousness (religious and moral rectitude in every area and relation) abides in our fruitful field (Isa. 33:2,6 AMP). The effect of righteousness is peace (internal and external), and the result of righteousness is quietness and confident trust forever.

Our family dwells in a peaceable habitation, in safe dwellings, and in quiet resting places. And there is stability in our times, abundance of salvation, wisdom, and knowledge (Isa. 32:15–18 AMP). Their reverent fear and worship of the Lord is our treasure and Yours, O Lord. Be gracious to us, Lord; we have waited (expectantly) for You. Be the arm of Your servants, our strength and defense every morning, our salvation in the time of trouble. Father, we thank You for our peace, our safety, and our welfare this day. Hallelujah!

In Jesus' name, Amen.

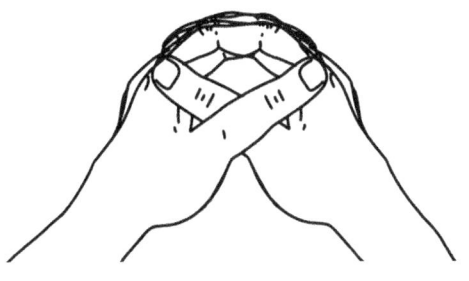

Psalm 91

Apostle Artherrine Grimes Hoskins

(Insert person's name you are praying for) _____ lives in the shadow of the almighty, sheltered by the God who is above all gods. _(name of person praying here.)_ declares that God alone is _____'s refuge, __(his/her)____ place of safety: He is _____'s God, and _____ is trusting Him. For God rescues _____from every trap and protects ___(him/her)_____ from the fatal plague. He will shield _____ with His wings. They will shelter _____. God's faithful promises are _____'s armor. Now _____ does not need to be afraid of the dark anymore, nor fear the dangers of the day; nor dread the plagues of darkness, nor disasters in the morning. Though a thousand fall at _____'s side, though ten thousand are dying around _____ these evils will not touch _____. _____ will see how the wicked are punished but __(he/she)_____will not share it. For Jehovah is _____'s refuge! _____ chooses the God above all gods to shelter __ (him/her)_____. How then can evil overtake _____ or any plague come near? For God orders His angels to protect _____ wherever __(he/she)___ goes. They will steady _____ with their hands to keep _(him/her)___ from stumbling against the rocks on the trail.

_____ can safely meet a lion or step on poisonous snakes, yes, even trample them beneath ___(his/her)_____feet! For the Lord says, "Because _____ loves Me, I will rescue _____ (him/her)_____; I will make _____ great because _(he/she)_____ trusts in My name. When _____ calls on Me I will answer; I will be with _(him/her)_____ in trouble. I will rescue and honor _____. I will satisfy _____ with a full life and give _____ My salvation.

In Jesus' name, Amen.

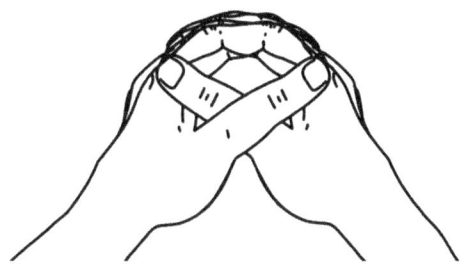

Eternal Life Prayer

Power of Agreement Global Prayer Network

"For God so loved the world, that he gave his only begotten Son, that whosoever believeth in him should not perish, but have everlasting life." —John 3:16

Heavenly Father, Thank You for sending Jesus to die for me. I come to You now acknowledging You as our God the creator of Heaven and Earth. Father, I forgive anyone who has ever done anything or said anything negative to me. I ask You to forgive and bless them, in Jesus' name. I ask You to forgive me for anything I have done toward others.

I believe in my heart that Jesus Christ is Your Son and that You sent Him to earth, and He was born of a virgin. I believe that Jesus Christ is the one true sacrifice for my sins. I accept Jesus as being the living bread which came down from heaven and as I partake of Him, I know that I shall live forever.

I believe that You raised Your Son Jesus from the dead and He is alive and well and seated at Your right hand in heaven. Heavenly Father, I plead the blood of Jesus over myself and thank You for the wonderful gift of salvation. I also ask You for Your other gift, the gift of the Holy Spirit. Lord fill me with Your Holy Spirit.

Thank You, Lord Jesus, for giving me the Holy Spirit according to Acts 15:8. Thank You, Father, for anointing me with the Holy Spirit and with Your power. Thank You for baptizing me with Your Holy Spirit and with fire according to Luke 3:16 so my life will glorify You. Thank You, Father, for faith and my salvation. I

51

believe Your Word, Father, and I accept Your promise of eternal life according to John 3:16.

Thank You for forgiving all my sins, thank You for the gift of salvation, thank You for the gift of the Holy Spirit, thank You for giving me the assurance that I will meet Jesus in peace.

In Jesus' name, Amen.

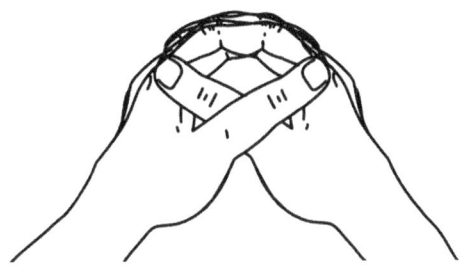

Prayer for Marriages

Anonymous

Lord, we are praying for and lifting up marriages (state names) to You. We pray that bonds will be strengthened as couples place You at the head of their lives (1 Cor.11:3) and their marriage. We pray for every union, that it would grow stronger and stronger each day. Father, we ask that You strengthen the marriage covenant and draw husbands and wives closer in love and unity.

Thank You, God, for sending divine mates. We decree and declare that the marriages we are praying for are of one flesh according to Genesis 2:24 and nothing shall be able to separate them from loving, caring for, and supporting each other. Father, remind husbands and wives to love each other; help them to be patient and kind, generous, and humble. Let them love and honor each other daily.

Teach them to be selfless and not self-seeking. Help them to walk in forgiveness each day, keeping no record of wrongs. Let them speak truth. We pray that they love each other unconditionally, as love protects and always trusts. Love always hopes and always perseveres (1 Cor. 13:4-7). We pray that spouses will allow love to lead them in their marriage as love never fails (1 Cor. 13:8).

Father, keep the love between husbands, wives, and their marriages fresh and new. Remind them of how they met and the love and joy they experienced. Take them back to the beginning to propel them forward for many years of love, joy, and happiness.

Lord, we pray that spouses surrender everything back to You. When tempted to do wrong, during disagreements, times of anger, and loneliness, we pray they will resist the devil and draw near to You. Show them Your way of love daily. Help them to love each other. Help them to honor and respect the gift of marriage.

Lord, we pray for peace in marriages. Help spouses to communicate better with each other. Give them wisdom. Let them seek You when making personal decisions, as well as decisions about their children and family. Father, search the hearts of husbands and wives and show them where they may need improvement. Let them seek Your Word for spiritual guidance. Lord, we pray that marriages be held in honor according to Hebrews 13:4. Lord, help spouses to submit to one another out of reverence for Christ. Help wives submit to their husbands as to the Lord and help husbands love their wives just as Christ loved the church (Eph. 5:21-25).

In Jesus' name, Amen.

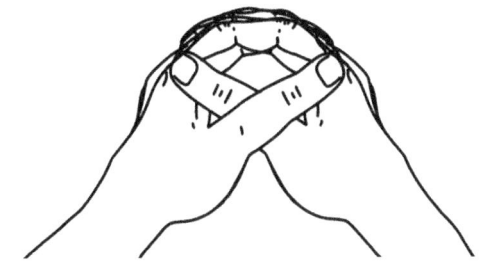

Prayer for Mothers (1 of 2)

Warrior Mother Kathleen Talley

"Train up a child in the way he should go, and when he is old, he will not depart from it."
— Proverbs 22:6 NKJV

Dear Heavenly Father,
We thank You for giving us the gift of our children. As mothers we also thank You for giving us the instructions in Your Word on how to raise our children in the reverence and admonition of the Lord.

Lord, help us so we will be able to continue to raise our children according to Your commands in Your Holy Word. May it always be the priority in our lives to live according to Your Son Jesus' example of obedience and honor to Your will as stated in Your Word. In the powerful name of Jesus Christ our Lord and Savior, I pray.

In Jesus' name, Amen.

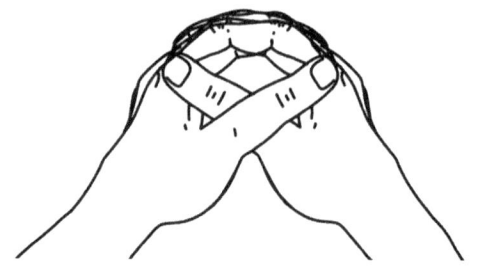

Prayer for Mothers (2 of 2)

Warrior Mother Gloria Wigfall

D ear Father,
   I thank You for the opportunity You've given me, the gift You've given all mothers, the gift of being a mom.

Dear Lord, being mothers, help us from time-to-time to just stop and reflect on the many ways You've come through for us. The way You have helped us during the times when we felt, in our minds, so worn and torn that we wanted to give up on our children, knowing full well in our hearts, that we would never ever give up on them. That, as mothers, we were willing and ready to go even beyond the last mile for them.

Father, I thank You that You give us wisdom to rest in You as You replenish our souls. Strengthen us so we can continue a little farther each day, until we witness our children grow into awesome young men and women of God, conditioned to go out and face the world. Father, even after they've reached adulthood, we're still moms. We still thank You and will forever praise You for covering them day-by-day with Your precious blood.

So, Father, I thank You for the overflowing love, strength, and faith You've given—and will continue to give—us to face each day, and the courage to walk on, no matter what.

Guide our thoughts so that we continue to walk in peace and in gratitude for the honor of being mothers.

I pray, "Above all else, guard your heart, for everything you do flows from it" (Prov. 4:23 NIV).

In Jesus' name, Amen.

Powerful Popcorn Prayers

Mother Apostle Artherrine Grimes Hoskins

Popcorn prayers are prayers you can pray anywhere and anytime. They are quick, powerful, and seasoned with God's Word!

Prayer of Praise

Father, I take this time to magnify, praise, and exalt Thy holy name, because You are worthy to be praised (Ps. 145:1); therefore, I will bless You, O Lord, at all times and Your praises shall continually be in my mouth (Ps. 34:1). I thank You, Father, that You are everything to me for You have revealed Yourself to me through Your Word as Jehovah, the great I AM, for You are everything I need.

In Jesus' name, Amen.

Prayer of Confession

Father God, I ask You to search and cleanse me of everything that displeases You with the blood of Jesus. Create in me a clean heart and renew a steadfast spirit within me. Restore to me the joy of Your salvation and sustain me with a willing spirit according to Psalm 51:10, 12.

In Jesus' name, Amen.

Prayer for Generations

Father God, I pray that Your purpose for the next generation will be fulfilled. I decree that the next generation will arise in power, authority, and influence to possess the gates of their enemies according to Genesis 22:17-18.

In Jesus' name, Amen.

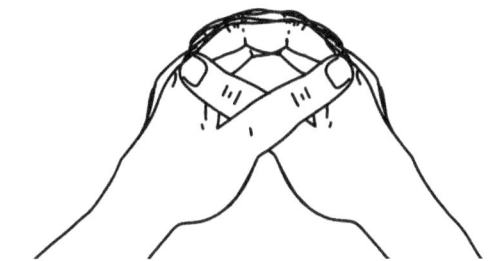

Prayer for Children and Youth

Warrior Pastor Chris Annan

Lord, thank You for all the children and the young people who love You, Lord, and have accepted You as their Lord and Savior. Please continue to draw near to them, as they have taken a leap of faith toward You, God (John 6:44). Father, continue to guide their steps, as they walk through this world (Ps. 37:23–24). Father, never leave nor forsake them (Heb. 13:5).

In challenging times, may they seek Your face, God, and not try to rely on their own understanding (Ps. 27:8, Prov 3:5–6). Lord, also please save Your children whose souls are lost. Give those who are out there contemplating their salvation peace, comfort, and protection.

Father, wherever they may be, as many as come forth, Father, alter their life course. Lead them to Your salvation. God, let them develop a spirit of humility, God, so they may know that the fear of God is the beginning of their wisdom (Prov. 9:10).

Lord, also give Your children the strength and understanding needed to always fight the good fight; to always keep their faith, and to always finish everything they start.

Lastly, God, I pray they will always be at the right place at the right time, with the right people, doing the right things.

In Jesus' name, Amen.

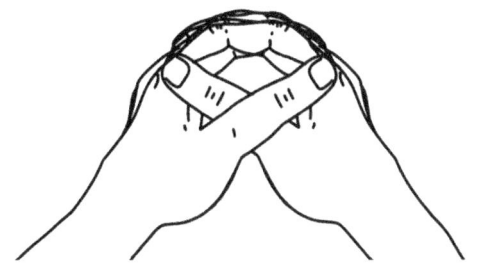

Prayer for Adult Children

Apostle Mother Artherrine Grimes Hoskins

Father, in the name of Jesus, we bring our adult children before the throne of grace.

First of all, we ask You to forgive us for the times we have prayed for them with selfish motives and hindered Your answers to prayer. Forgive us for our self-righteous attitudes. Father, help us stay mindful that it was not too long ago that we were bound in an old stagnant life of sin, but You embraced us with mercy, grace, and love.

Thank You for the blessing of each child You have given us and for their unique purpose and destiny in life. We commit them to You and ask You to intervene in their lives at every opportunity today, revealing Your wonderful nature in new and fresh ways. Shine Your heavenly light into areas of darkness and lead them on paths of righteousness and peace. We thank You for the infusion of the Holy Spirit in their lives through love, the fruit of the Spirit, for wisdom and revelation, and the knowledge of You, Father God.

Create pure hearts in our children and renew a right spirit within them according to Psalm 51:10. Nehemiah 4:14 tells us to fight for our children! Father, You are great and awesome and worthy to be praised. We fight for our sons, daughters, our spouses, and our houses in Jesus' name. We thank You that Your promises are "yes" and "amen," and that You will contend with those who contend with us. And You will give safety to our children, save them, and ease them day-by-day. You are our LORD, our Savior, our Redeemer, and our Rock! (Ps. 18:1-2).

Help our children choose their friends. Please keep them from ungodly relationships. Give them keen discernment. May they hear Your voice and be quick to listen. May all our children repent and be baptized in the name of the Lord Jesus Christ for the remission of sins and receive the gift of the Holy Spirit (Acts 2:38-39). Thank You for pouring out Your Holy Spirit upon our adult children now so they can prophesy; so our young men will see visions according to Your Word in Acts 2:17. Father, create in them a love for Your Word, Your Holy Scripture. Fill their lives with Your presence and guide their steps daily. Thank You, dear Father, that our children are a chosen generation, a royal priesthood, and a holy nation. Thank You, Father, for confirming Your Word in them. We give You glory, honor, and praise.

In Jesus' name, Amen.

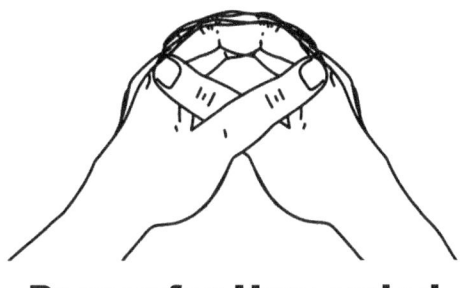

Prayer for Unmarried

Warrior Minister Desmarie Guyton-Babb

Lord, as I come to You, my Father who is in heaven, I humble myself at Your feet, as Ruth did with Boaz, asking and thanking You for covering me. I thank You, Lord, that although I am not married in the natural, I am Your bride in the spiritual who lacks nothing, for You provide all my needs. You are mine and I am Yours, and Your love is the greatest love I have ever known; love that provides me comfort when I'm alone, yet I'm not lonely.

It is love that catches every tear when circumstances of this world have caused me to cry out to You. It is love that has given His life for me, died for me, and rose again for me so that I may be set free and have a life with You, my Savior, as Your bride.

I'm so grateful for Your love, and as I live in this world that is not my home, I ask You, Jesus, to keep me, Your bride, in the protection of You. Continue to lead me on Your path of righteousness, so I'm not like silly women or men being led by fleshly desires or emotions that can bring me to the pitfalls of this world. I ask instead to be constantly led by Your Holy Spirit, leading me beside Your still waters that bring restoration to my soul.

Let the refreshment of Your Holy Spirit continue to bring forth living water in my life as it pours out Your love for all to see. And let others stand in awe of Your beauty, my husband, my Lord, and my Savior. You have bestowed Your image upon me, giving me Your name.

Thank You for Your love. Thank You for Your wisdom. Thank You for all You have given me, Your bride. I will honor You and continue to give You all the glory now and forever.

In Jesus' name, Amen.

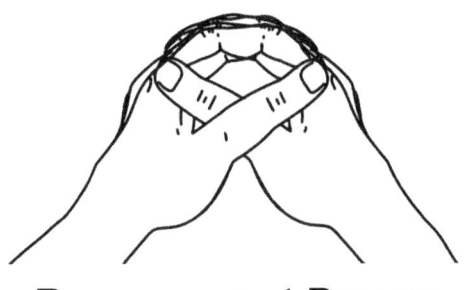

Bereavement Prayer

Dr. Peggy Enochs

2 Corinthians 1:3–7

To a most wise, loving, and caring Father, we honor You and bless Your name. Thank You, Lord, that You are present with us today. Thank You that we can cast all our cares upon You. Thank You that You are touched by our infirmities. Thank You that You had a plan for our lives even before we were born. Thank You for the price You paid that we might have an abundant life. Thank You that You went to heaven to prepare a place for us. Thank You, Christ in us; You are the hope of glory!

Today, dear Father, we come to You on behalf of individuals, families, and friends who have lost loved ones through death. Maybe it was a sudden death. Maybe it was a natural death. Perhaps there was a chronic or acute illness, or maybe, it was death by suicide. It could have been a stillbirth, an abortion, a miscarriage, a murder, or even the death of a pet. Maybe some had to make a difficult medical decision for a loved one that ended in termination of life. Whatever the case, their heart is fractured; the grief is hard.

The pain is great, and at times, one feels as an overwhelming tangled ball of emotions. Some are devastated and numb. Thank You, Lord, for the assurance that they are never alone in their state of sorrow, despair, or grief. You too have experienced grief. In the Garden of Gethsemane, You felt overwhelming sadness and anguish and asked the Father, "If it is possible, let this cup pass from me" (Matt. 26:39). You even wept when Lazarus died (John 11:35). You know pain and sorrow. We thank You for the gift of being able to cry and release—to let go and to find comfort in a wise and all-knowing God. And, for those who have shattered beliefs about life, the world, and even God, meet them at their point of need.

Thank You, Lord, for the Holy Spirit, the great Comforter, our compassionate Helper, and Companion, who will lead us through this healing journey as we call on Your great name. Thank You, Lord, that weeping may endure for a night, but joy comes in the morning. Lord, send people across the paths of those grieving to bring divine comfort.

May they choose God's Word and speak truth. May they know that it's okay to be silent. Yes, their presence can mean so much more than many words. Send people given to acts of kindness, and people who will follow through for months after the initial loss. We thank You, Lord, for the heavy lifters who can assist one another with heart-heavy burdens of all kinds. We thank You, Lord, for the praying saints and for our great Intercessor for making intercession on their behalf.

For the bereaved, Lord, continue to surround them with Your overwhelming love, strength, truth, rest, and peace that surpasses all understanding. Thank You, Lord, for new mercies every day. Thank You, Lord, that Your compassion refreshes and refills every morning as You bring more mercy and grace into their lives. You hear their cries, and You feel their pain. You can also see deep within their heart.

Have Your way, Lord! May they have a heart of gratitude, even in their deepest sorrows. Cause them to think and ponder on the good times experienced with their loved one and give thanks. May they be given a good dose of medicine—laughter—for it will bring healing for the spirit, soul, and body through the releasing of stress, improving their mood, boosting immunity, and relieving pain.

And, Father, add a "now" word to encourage them to press their way through the maze of emotions in this journey toward divine freedom. Let them hear Your voice above the silence, the noise, and the pain. Many things they may question or not understand about the death of their loved one. May You rid them of the "woulda, coulda, shouldas" that could bring heartache and regrets. May they focus on Your character and who You are, the Great I AM. May they release their fractured hearts to You, loving and faithful God.

I pray, God, that they would not separate themselves from You, Father. Satan cannot steal their destiny. May their eyes be opened as their gaze and hearts are fixed upon You so they will walk this journey of healing out to Your glory.

Thank You, Lord, that there is no failure in You. Help them, Lord, to look past the pain to see Your glorious face clearly and unmistakably. May they be reminded that Your plans are good for them, not to harm them, but to give them a future and a hope. May they awaken in this hour to the provisions You have already made for their healing.

In Jesus' name, Amen.

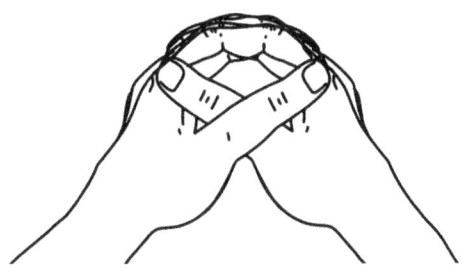

Prayer for Widows
A Widow's Journey

Warrior Gloria Towner

When first starting on this "journey of widowhood," a life filled with unexpected changes and challenges, one is so stunned and numb. There is uncertainty regarding what to do or expect. As Christians, we believe and trust God. However, widows must go through the grief process. Part of that process is anger. Yes, being angry with God for taking your loved one, is part of the process. But we do not stay there long. Many of us will also rationalize and bargain with God before actually recognizing that God is love, and God loves us!

God so loved the world that He gave His only Son to die for us (John. 3:16). When we accept this truth again, then we begin to understand, accept, and feel empowered to pray and to believe. God loved your husband, who also believed, so much that he is not dead. He lives because of God's Son, Jesus Christ. It is at this time that we will likely begin talking to God, finding, and reading words of encouragement, opening up our Bibles, and commencing a journey of prayer, praise, and trusting God, which may include writing a journal.

The Lord's Prayer and Psalm 23 usually become familiar points of reference, and they bring great comfort. These Scriptures begin, for many (as they did for me), a sustaining foundation for strengthening a personal relationship with God. The following prayer encompasses my early days, months, and years of learning to pray. I would talk to God, tell Him what was happening to me, and seek His guidance. I would thank and praise Him as I trusted Him to keep me and bring me back to a life of living again!

The Prayer

Father God, in the name of Jesus, I come before You. First Lord, I want to thank You for getting me through another day. Thank You for the life my husband and I had together. Thank You for blessing and keeping us through the great times, good times, and the bad times. Thank You, Lord, for Your grace, goodness, and mercy.

Lord, I know Your Word says You will comfort those who mourn, that You are my Shepherd, and I shall not want; that You sent Your Word to heal the brokenhearted, and You would never leave nor forsake me. I believe Your goodness and mercy will follow me all the days of my life. But Lord, right now I feel so heavy and burdened. My heart is broken. It feels like a part of it has been cut away and I am feeling numb and alone. I have people around me who are praying and trying to encourage me. I thank You for them. But Lord this is me (insert your name) talking to You, my Father. I am trying to express some of the emotions I am feeling. I know Scripture says to cast all my cares on You, for You care for me.

I need to feel Your loving care. I need to feel Your presence, Holy Spirit. I feel lost and alone without my husband (name). Lord, I feel empty, devastated, and tired. I feel like my own life has come to a stop, a dry place. Yet, I am crying wet tears and trying to smile at the same time.

I am thankful for the friends and family who are trying to encourage me, telling me everything is going to be alright. Lord, I know You are God and Lord over my life. You know what it is like to see someone You love die! After all, You gave Your only Son, Jesus Christ, to die for us. Lord, I know because of Christ, death is not the end for those who believe. And I do believe You God and trust You.

I believe in Jesus, who said to Mary and Martha, when their brother died, that He, Jesus, is the resurrection! Because of Christ, I can and will have the strength to endure and live an eternal life with You! Right now, Lord, I need You to take my hand and uphold me with Your righteous right hand. Pull me out of this valley and uphold me! Lift me up out of this miry clay, out of the valley of grief.

I believe, Father, You will bring me out of this grief. You have done it for others, and I know You are no respecter of persons. I believe You are my Jehovah Jireh, my provider; You can do anything but fail. I believe Your Word that says:

• You will turn my mourning into dancing (Psalm30:11).

• You will take off this heavy garment of grief and restore it with praise (Psalms 30:11).

• You will never leave me nor forsake me (Deuteronomy 31:6).

• And You will give me joy for my sorrow (Jeremiah 31:13).

Holy Spirit, my helper, help me make this exchange of restoration right now, in the name of Jesus! Lord, help me also understand all the business, paperwork, insurance, and the estate matters. Please send honest and compassionate people who will assist my family and me. Thank You, God, for meeting all our needs according to Your riches and glory through Christ Jesus.

Lord, as I place all these things in Your care, I am already feeling the presence of Your spirit and power. Thank You for being such a loving and attentive God. Thank You for Your peace and fresh anointing. To God be the glory. I love You, Lord. I thank You, Lord. I praise You, Lord God.

In Jesus' name, Amen.

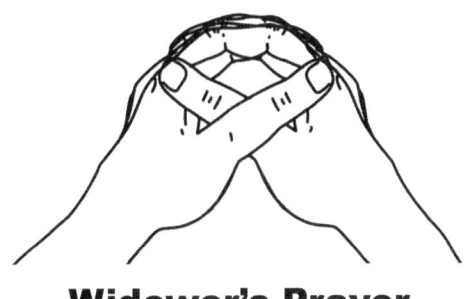

Widower's Prayer

Warrior Rolene Love

Lord, I thank You for Your peace and comfort. When I go through trials and struggles and can barely see ahead, You are already there with me. You lift me above my circumstances to a place of comfort and direction.

I thank You, Lord, that when I go through difficult times You will give me a greater sense of Your comfort. I know You are my refuge and strength. Lord, You are the light of my life and a lamp unto my feet that can never be put out. No matter what I face in life, the Holy Spirit is there to help me and to direct my path.

Lord, I give You thanks in all things, knowing that You reign in the midst of it all, and that God shall supply all my needs according to His riches in Glory by Christ Jesus (Phil. 4:19).

In times of trials, Lord I pray for Your added sense of presence. I will now rest in confidence knowing, leaning, and believing in You, O Lord.

In Jesus' name, Amen.

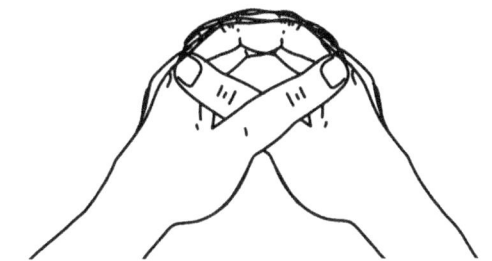

Prayer for Unresolved Grief

Pastor DeBorah Holt-Foster

Our Mother, Our Father, Our Everything God,
We call You our All because You are all things to us and over all things. Grief is an experience of sorrow and distress that each of us will eventually face in our lifetime. Grief alters our lives, but over time, it eases so we can return to our reality without pain. Yes, Lord, there are many whose emotional pain will not cease. There are those who suffer from unresolved grief.

Psalm 34:18 says, "The LORD is close to the brokenhearted and saves those who are crushed in spirit" (NIV). Lord, help the brokenhearted see that grief is a process only You can help them overcome. Lord, help them understand that we are created in Your likeness, and as such, You know all about us and how we feel. Help us, Jesus, know and accept that when we place our weaknesses on You, that You will make us strong.

Scripture says in Matthew 5:4 that in my mourning I am blessed, and that in my mourning I will be comforted. Thank You, Father, that in the midst of my mourning I do receive Your blessings. Help me put my trust in You so You can direct me from my pain. Help me seek Your understanding in my pain. Lord, though my grief seems unbearable, I thank You for hearing my cries. I thank You for feeling my sorrow. I thank You for walking with me in the dark shadows so I may experience peace, joy, and light in place of grief.

Lord, allow my healing of tears sown to comfort others because I am reminded of what I sow in tears I shall reap in joy. Help me, Lord, accept that the life that I grieve was borrowed, that You love me so much that You are with me always. Thank You, Mother, Father, Everything God, for keeping me and strengthening me.

In Jesus' name, Amen.

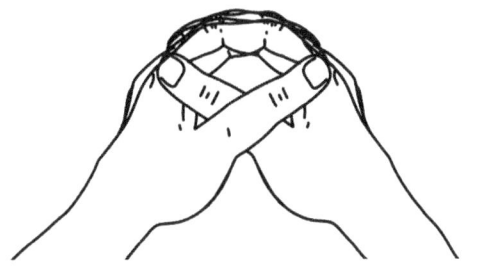

Prayer for Mental Health

Pastor DeBorah Holt-Foster

O Lord, our Gracious Father, we pause to say thank You for Your enduring love, grace, and mercy toward us. Heavenly Father, in times such as these, many are realizing they are falling under the weight of the world's pressures. In times like these, many are faced with fragile hearts, fragile bodies, and fragile minds. As our God of compassion, Lord, we ask that You deliver those whose minds are spinning with dysfunctional thoughts. We ask You, Lord, to deliver those who hear silent voices that tell them they are not good enough. Deliver them from silent voices that say that they will never amount to anything; that they are unworthy. Deliver all those who face mental challenges that were instilled at birth.

Lord, we pray that those whose minds are captured by ADD, ADHD, ASD, Asperger's syndrome, Alzheimer's disease, bipolar disorder, child neglect, cognition disorder, dementia, depression, Down syndrome, hysteria, mood disorder, narcolepsy, pedophiliac disorder, schizophrenia, sleep paralysis, Tourette's syndrome, and all other mental disorders, that You control their brain function with order and understanding.

Help each of us to rely on Your Word in Isaiah 41:10, "Do not fear, for I am with you; Do not anxiously look about you, for I am your God. I will strengthen you, surely I will help you, Surely I will uphold you with My righteous right hand" (NASB).

Father, sustain them; lift up lowered heads. Destroy shame and isolation. Heal, in the name of Jesus, injured minds today.

Father, when we feel overwhelmed with racing thoughts, closed throats, sleeplessness, loneliness, and anxiety, remind us that Jesus loves us in spite of us because He knew what abandonment felt like. He accepted the cups of abuse and trauma. He promised to never leave us alone.

In Jesus' name, Amen.

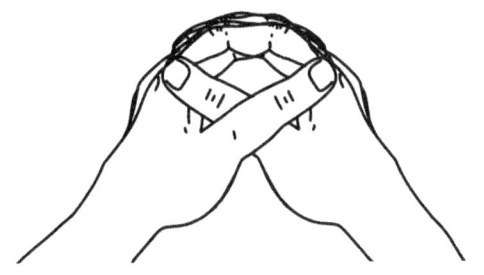

Prayer for Female Clergy

Warrior Pastor Pamela G. Kellar

Almighty Creator, Thou who made heaven and earth. Thou who has brought us thus far on our way. Thou who has appointed us to serve You in a more excellent way. We praise and give thanks to You.

We thank You for strength and pray You will grant us wisdom. We thank You, O God, for those You provided to us as mentors and friends. We thank You for our forerunners upon whose shoulders we stand, who listened to Your call and turned a deaf ear to naysayers.

We pray for female clergy, Your women in ministry. Fortify us, Lord God, in Your grace, mercy, and love. Teach us Your ways and lead us along a straight path. Teach us, God, to act justly, to love mercy, and to walk humbly with You.

Expand our understanding of what it means to worship You, so our worship translates to service to mankind. Open our hearts to be doers of the Word of God by caring for those in need, by speaking for our brothers and sisters who are voiceless, and to decree charity to the disenfranchised and marginalized.

Help us, O God, to not become oppressors to each other because of pettiness and jealousy. Instead, teach us to become a chain not easily broken. Let us become a chain linked in love, joy, peace, patience, kindness, goodness, faithfulness, gentleness, self-control, and respect according to Your Word in Galatians 5:22-23, so we can be a blessing to You and Your kingdom. We present these petitions asking in the mighty and matchless name of Jesus. Amen and Ashay.*

*Ashay is a word used in African American culture to mean "and so it is" or "Amen."

In Jesus' name, Amen.

Prayer for Clergy

Pastor DeBorah Holt-Foster

Precious Lord, Our Heavenly Father and Creator,
We offer ourselves to You, O God, and we thank You for being Your chosen vessels. We seek Your blessings today on our clergy, pastors, ministers, and priests, who are picked out to lead Your people into the way in which they should go. We thank You, Lord God, for loving the world so much that You gave Your Son to the world for redemption.

We thank You for those who give of their time, talent, and treasure to be the leaders of today facing the storms of tomorrow. We thank You, Lord, for those who were called who said, "yes" to Your will and to Your way. Lord, grant our clergy the quality time needed to pray and to study Your holy Scripture.

Grant them the wisdom to minister, to counsel, and to love on those who are hurting, lonely, helpless, wounded, broken, disappointed, despised, and rejected. Help them offer hope to people who have lost hope, peace to people in chaos, and comfort to people in grief and strife.

Father, give them patience when visiting the sick, feeding the hungry, guiding the ministries and/or church, and in praying without compromising Your holy name.

Give them the boldness to declare Your Word in these end times with signs and wonders. Release Your anointing upon them as in the days of Pentecost. Set a fire down in their souls that cannot be contained when they preach, reach, and teach. Consume by fire, God, every satanic power and devices standing in opposition against the preaching of the gospel, in the name of Jesus.

Arm them with the gift of discernment to challenge the unhealthy values of our culture. Provide our clergy times of rest and spiritual refreshment. Help others to be sensitive to the impossible time demands they may place on them. Give them the freedom to say, "NO!" to temptation and to those things that might diminish their ability to minister well.

Protect our clergy, Lord, in all aspects of ministry from the evil forces that oppose Your kingdom. Set solid boundaries of respect concerning their need for time with family, for privacy, and for rest. Make us slow to criticize but quick to love and encourage.

Father, give them the shield of faith and the sword of the Spirit. Protect their health, their families, their reputations, their finances, and their moral resolve. When they are tempted, Lord, be their refuge and help. You are their strength, so when they give in to temptation, lead them into forgiveness and restoration that will better equip them to comprehend and share the depth of Christ's redeeming love.

Help others to be slow to judge, to criticize, to have anger with our clergy, yet be quick to love and encourage. Help our clergy, pastors, ministers, priests, and ministry leaders avoid being critical of one another.

Acts 20:28 reads, "Keep watch over yourselves and all the flock of which the Holy Spirit has made you overseers. Be shepherds of the church of God, which he bought with his own blood."

In Jesus' name, Amen.

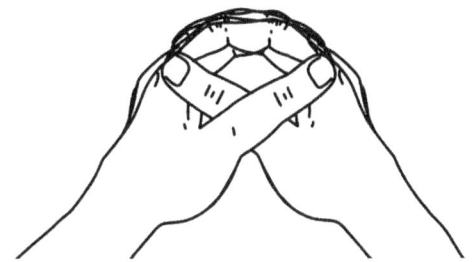

Prayer for the Office of the President

Warrior Althea Ledford

Lord, bless the Office of the President of our country. Bless the current president as an individual and the Office of the President as a standing space to be occupied by all future presidents. Let these prayers extend into the future and for the duration of this country. Bless this office to operate with clean hands, clean hearts, keen minds, listening ears, and in total awareness to the presence of the Lord.

Let the cabinet members look and represent all nationalities, men and women, and all age groups. As the age groups come together let them utilize the elders' wisdom and the quickness and new knowledge of our youth.

Bless all cabinet members and staff. Let the staff be wise and timely as the five wise virgins, thinking of alternative solutions and plans without being asked. May they be quick to step up and step in as needed, working wholeheartedly for the benefit of the nation without ego or personal agendas.

Let this office and all future offices work to achieve bipartisanship at all levels, as this benefits our country and both parties move toward a more God-conscious nation.

Bless the plans and all future plans of the Office of the President. Ensure planning is done with the spirit of discernment. If any harmful wording is buried, covertly placed, or hidden in any document, let it always be sourced out and revealed.

Squash and destroy the plans of the enemy at the root. Destroy any plans to sabotage or plant seeds of fear, doubt, confusion, misgivings, miscommunication, direct lies, and anything that contradicts the will of God.

Let the Office of the President be refreshed spiritually. Let the oil used to polish and the cloths used to dust, serve a dual duty of reanointing this office with Your presence daily.

Finally, Lord, we pray that You hover over this and all future presidents. That Your will be done always and this nation stay "One nation under God indivisible with liberty and justice for all."[11]

In Jesus' name, Amen.

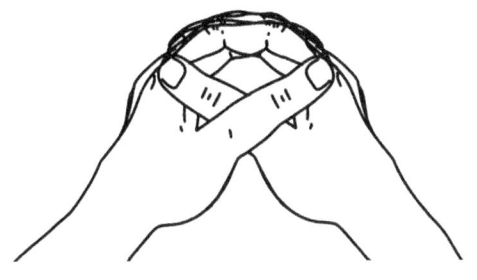

Prayer for the State

Warrior Minister Crystal Bouldin

1 Timothy 2:1–4, Matthew 16:19

I pray in the name of Jesus for every man, woman, and child living in this state. From mountain top to valley low to every home, business, marketplace, church, mall, city hall, government and government agencies, parks, and land in the state. We release the wisdom of God to fulfill Your plan in the earth and bless the people that we, the body of Christ, may live a quiet and peaceable life in all godliness and honesty. We lift up the state and our community unto You and declare total and absolute victory over the works of darkness.

Satan, I bind you and command you to take your hands off this state and this community. Take your hands off the social, political, and economic arenas.

I let loose the power of God to accomplish the will of God in the land. As You taught us to pray, "Thy kingdom come, Thy will be done" (Matt. 6:10) in this state as it is in heaven.

In Jesus' name, Amen.

.

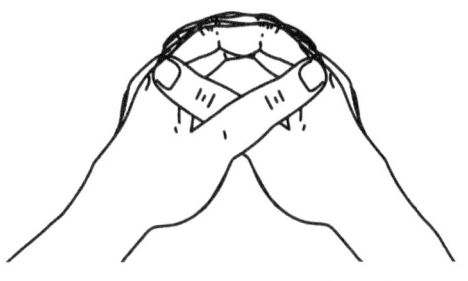

Prayer for the Nation

Warrior Minister Crystal Bouldin

2 Chronicles 7:14–15, Ephesians 3:20

In the name of Jesus, I lift this great nation in prayer. This country was founded on the pursuit of freedom, liberty, justice, and in God we trust.[2] We, Your people come before You, Lord, in humility to pray and seek Your face. In agreement with Your Word, we pray for this nation to turn from its wicked ways so then You will hear from heaven, forgive their sin, and heal this nation.

You are our God, Almighty God, God of all the earth, Creator of heaven and earth, and are able to do infinitely more than we ask or imagine. We stir up the power that worketh in us on behalf of this nation for an awesome move of Your Spirit to disrupt, intervene, block, and stop the enemy and his evil work in this nation. "From sea to shining sea,"[3] from north to south and east to west we release Your glory, Your power, Your goodness, and Your mercy. "For thine is the kingdom and the power and the glory forever" (Matt. 6:13).

In Jesus' name, Amen.

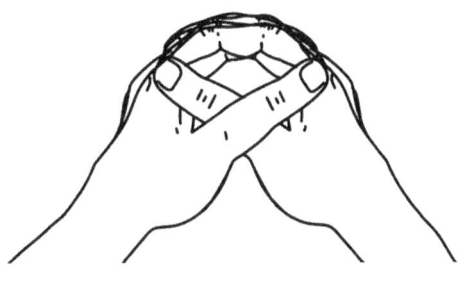

Prayer for the Nations

Minister Yolanda E. Shields
Author, Speaker, CEO

Heavenly Father,
We pray and intercede with thanksgiving for all nations and people, including those in high positions of power in local and national government and other positions of authority.

Lord, we pray that You would look down in grace and mercy on all nations. Guide them in Your grace that they may honor You in their nation, so they may live a quiet, peaceful, and godly life that is honoring to You. Father, we ask You to give wisdom to those responsible for making decisions to establish national and local laws.

Lord, we ask that You intervene in the decisions made in high places, and we especially pray that You would frustrate discussions and decisions made in secret places that are outside of Your desires for all nations.

We disrupt the plans of men and women who wish evil, and we pray they instead make plans for Your greater good and for the benefit of those whom they serve.

Raise up a generation in all nations that will serve You. Lord, give us an opportunity to serve nations because Your Word says, "Ask me, and I will make the nations your inheritance, the ends of the earth your possession" (Ps. 2:8 NIV). We praise and thank You.

In Jesus' name, Amen.

Prayer for Israel

Warrior Sharon Mitchell

Out of reverence for devout Jews who will neither speak nor write the ineffable holy name of God but would rather print it like this—G-d, I do the same in this prayer.

Prayer for Repentance and Salvation for the Jewish People

We thank You, Abba (Father), for Abraham and his descendants, Your chosen people. You chose Abraham and his descendants, the Jewish people, because Abraham chose You! "He believed in the Lord (Adonai) and he credited it to him as righteousness" (Gen. 15:6 emphasis mine).

May we Jews repent, forsake pride, and understand that it was only through Abraham's faithfulness and Your lovingkindness that we were chosen. We thank You, Abba, that we were chosen for covenant with You, to be a light to the nations of the world (Deut. 14:2; Isa. 42:6), and to have Messiah Yeshua (Jesus Christ), the true light of the world (John 1:4, 9), come through our lineage for the salvation of all mankind. (Rom. 11:17; 1 Kings 2:45; Matt. 1:1–1; Rom. 10:9–11). What a privilege!

We repent for not having recognized, taken offense, rejected, and even disparaged our Messiah who came to us first (Rom. 1:16). As Yeshua said, "Father, forgive them; for they know not what they do" (Luke 23:34 KJV).

We agree with Your plan, Abba, that "all Israel shall be saved" (Rom. 11:26). As the time of the "fullness of the gentiles" is unfolding

91

(Rom. 11:25–27), we pray that any scales fall off our spiritual eyes, and You touch our minds and hearts to know You and gain a clear understanding of who our Messiah is, gain an understanding of His purpose and true identity in You. May we grow to recognize, honor, and love You, Yeshua (Jesus), "Arm of G-d" (Isa. 52:10), who became the "Lamb of G-d" and made propitiation for all of our sins (John 1:29; Rev. 1:8; Isa. 53). May we come to know the dual roles of our Messiah as both the "suffering servant" and the "conquering king" (Isa. 53; Rev. 19:11), "the one who is, who was and who is coming" (Rev. 1:8).

Prayer for the Peace of Jerusalem and Unity Within Her Walls

"Pray for shalom (peace) in Yerushalayim (Jerusalem); may those who love you prosper" (Ps. 122:6). In the name of Yeshua, Sar Shalom (Prince of Peace), we speak shalom to Israel's borders. We call forth shalom and godly unity within her borders among her diverse citizenry: Jews, Christians, Muslims, and all who reside there (Ps. 147:14). May the Israeli governmental and political leaders find deeper understanding and new ways to work together for the good of the nation. May they fully understand that a house divided cannot stand (Mark 3:25).

In the name of Yeshua, we cut the lies of the enemy with the sword of the Spirit and demolish all demonic strongholds of falsehood, witchcraft, offense, indoctrination, bigotry, anti-Semitism, hatred, murder, and all blood vendettas (Eph. 6:12; Luke 10:19). We call forth reconciliation, through Your grace, of the Jewish people with all Gentiles, Christians, Arabs, and Muslims. "When a man's ways please Adonai (Lord), he makes even his enemies be at peace with him" (Prov. 16:7 ESV emphasis mine).

We call forth the revelation of the One True G-d, sincere repentance, heart changes, love, understanding, and unity among all people to bring forth an increased authentic, beautiful, multicultural Bride of Christ. Amen.

Prayer for the Israeli Government, Military, and Society

We thank You, Adonai, that godly watchmen including Israeli citizens, the leadership, government, and military are vigilant and aware on every level, that we hear from Your Ruach HaKodesh (Holy Spirit or "Breath of G-d"), and heed Your directives and warnings. We thank You that "the guardian of Israel never slumbers or sleeps" (Ps. 121:4 NASB), and we give thanks for the many miraculous military victories for us over the millennia. We pray for wisdom, discernment, and godly strategies for the government and military of Israel, including her Prime Minister (currently _____), his cabinet, advisors, the Knesset (Congress), and all leaders in positions of power and influence in every area of Israeli society.

We thank You that Israel is a democratic republic (the only one in the Middle East at this time), and that she is a worldwide leader in medical breakthroughs, humanitarian advancements, and environmental and technological discoveries.

Prayer for Reconciliation between Christians and Jews

May my Jewish people come to understand that the atrocities committed against them over the millennia, under the banner of "Christianity," in the name of "Jesus," and by "Christian" nations, were not of You, Yeshua! May our misconceptions about true Christianity be cleared up. In March 1998, Pope John Paul II apologized to the Jewish people for the passivity of the Vatican during the Holocaust. We pray for increased appropriate public repentance and sincere apologies for anti-Semitic attitudes and behaviors including "replacement theology" (teaching that the Church has replaced Israel).

We especially repent for the lack of recognition and even outright opposition to Israel's biblical and historical right to the land, as ordained by You, Abba (Gen. 15:18–21).

May Your whole truth about the Middle East situation, in all its simplicity and complexity, come to light! May Christians and

Jews alike have the conviction, courage, and wisdom, under Your direction and blessing, to stand for Israel staunchly and effectively when required.

May my Jewish people begin to see with new eyes and forgive. May legitimate, earned trust between the Jewish people and Christians be established. May we Jews ask for forgiveness for our resentments, fears, and distrust of gentiles. May we learn to fully trust only in You, Adonai, our Rock, and our Redeemer (Ps. 146:3-7).

Prayer of Thanksgiving and Sealing

We thank You, Adonai, for the privilege to partner with You as Your intercessors on behalf of the Israel. We know You hear and answer our worthy prayers. We give thanks and will continue to pray for Israel in accordance with Your will. We thank You for blessing those who bless Israel! (Gen.12:3).

Shalom!

In Jesus' name, Amen.

Be Blessed

Apostle Mother Artherrine Grimes Hoskins

Now in closing, I want you to know that I love each of you and there is nothing you can do about it because this love is being birthed from the third heaven. To my husband, children, spiritual children, grandchildren, spiritual grandchildren, and children to come, nieces and nephews, sisters and brothers, all the writers in this book, all my sisters and brothers all over the world, and to every reader of this book, I love you and I bless you.

I pray for you and mention your name before the throne of grace every day. My most sincere prayer is that we all meet together with our Lord Jesus Christ. Stay close to Jesus and He will stay close to you. I pray for the bond of unity to be strong among us. I decree that any schisms and contentions among us will be broken quickly.

> *"The LORD bless you and keep you;*
> *The LORD make His face to shine upon you and be gracious to you;*
> *The LORD lift up His countenance upon you and give you peace."*
> — Numbers 6:24-26 (ESV)

In Jesus' name, Amen.

Acknowledgments

This is now my third publication. I am deeply grateful for everyone who assisted me in the completion of this book and am pleased to acknowledge them and their invaluable contributions. I would like to thank each warrior who contributed prayers for this project; Warrior Pastor Chris Annan, Warrior Minister Crystal Bouldin, Warrior Dr. Peggy Enochs, Warrior Catherine Floyd, Warrior Minister Desmarie Guyton-Babb, Warrior Pastor DeBorah Holt-Foster, Warrior Husband Harvey E. Hoskins, CPA, Warrior Gwelthalyn Huff, Warrior Pastor Terrell Hunt, Warrior Pastors Chris and Gina Inkum, Warrior Tangela M. Jones Grimes, Warrior Pastor Pamela G. Kellar, Warrior Prophet Mark Korley, Warrior Althea Ledford, Warrior Rolene Love, Warrior Connie Martin, Warrior Apostle Eugenie Angela Mayers, Warrior Sharon Mitchell, Warrior Jacqui Rogers, Warrior/Minister/Coach Yolanda E. Shields, Warrior Kathleen Talley, Warrior Gloria Towner, Warrior Patricia A. Walker, Warrior Gloria Wigfall, and Warrior Dr. Diana R. Williams.

I would like to extend my sincere gratefulness to Pastor Pamela G. Kellar and Reverend Dr. Diana R. Williams for contributing your design and layout skills and sharing your knowledge in printing/publishing during the first publication of the prayer guide.

Thank you, Dr. Peggy Enochs, for proofreading the prayers during the second publication of the prayer guide. A special thank you to Coach Yolanda E. Shields for guiding me through the ups and downs through book updates, editing, and publishing during the second publication of the prayer guide.

Thank you to my divine helpers, who have helped me in countless ways in each stage of development of this edition, Pastor DeBorah Holt-Foster, Warrior Jacqui Rogers, Warrior Catherine Floyd, Warrior Tangela M. Jones Grimes, Warrior Lue, Dr. Diana R. Williams, and Warrior Kathleen Talley. Thank you for your prayers and availability and patience. Thanks for your help with proofing and preparing documents in preparation to be submitted to the editor.

Now we are here. I was blessed to receive an answer to prayers when God connected me to Julie Castro and Fiesta Publishing. To

God be the glory! I thank Him for sending the right publisher at the right time with the right spirit, expertise, and knowledge. Julie and her team have patiently assisted and guided me through the process of designing, proofing, and editing the content of this third edition until the completion.

To all the prayer warriors for the Power of Agreement Global Prayer Network Ministry all over the United States, Africa (Ghana), Jamaica, Israel, Mexico, Switzerland, Bahamas, and Barbados that pray as a community of love and unity on the Power of Agreement prayer lines. Thank you for your prayers and participation.

Giving praise to the Heavenly Father for the following people that have impacted my prayer journey and ministry: My Great High Priest and perfect example of an intercessor, the Lord Jesus Christ, Charles Spurgeon, John and Charles Wesley, my parents, Arthur Lee and Frances Lowe Grimes, Dr. Myles Munroe, Prayer Warrior Eleanor Graves, Pastor Linda Blackman, Pastor Dr. Arthur Alexander, Pastor Renee Franklin, Apostle Kimberly Daniels, Mother Mary Mimms, Dr. Cindy Trimm, Prayer Warrior Germaine Copeland, Pastor Glen Clay, Apostle John Eckhardt, Pastors Chris and Gina Inkum, Prayer Warrior Stormie Omartian, Pastor/Dr. Diana Williams, Apostle Dr. Eugenie Mayers, Bishop Rice Brooks, Bishop Dr. Jackie L. Green, Pastor James Lowe, and Pastor Walter Willis.

All the above have mentored me through teachings, intercession, time, prophetic insight, books, or CDs. They have all had a positive effect on my life and calling as an intercessor.

I am deeply grateful for everyone who assisted me in the completion of this book and am pleased to acknowledge them and their invaluable contributions.

Finally, a special thanks to Reverend Willie and Mrs. Antonia McLaurin and the Tennessee Baptist Mission Board for your fervent prayers and generous support during the first and second editions.

About the Founder
The Power of Agreement
Global Prayer Network

Apostle Mother Artherrine Grimes Hoskins is a certified spiritual life coach. She is a dynamic and motivating inspirational speaker, trainer, and consultant workshop leader, a life changer, who desires to empower and coach women to different levels and dimensions of spiritual, personal, and professional success and achievement. She is the visionary, founder and overseer of the nonprofit organization Power of Agreement Global Prayer Network.

Evangelist Hoskins is a spiritual mother, prophetic intercessor, and prayer warrior. She served as a National Prayer Coordinator for the National Consortium of Black Women in Ministry (NCBWIM), which is the leading professional organization for black women in ministry in the United States.

She is also one of the prayer team leaders for Powerhouse Ministries. She received her pastoral psychotherapy and chaplaincy instructions under the certification of Rev. Richard Reeves and Dr. Sandy Powell in 2010. On June 27, 2021, Evangelist Artherrine Grimes Hoskins was ordained, set, and sent as an apostle of prayer and mother in Zion by Bishop Dr. Jackie L. Green, by the authority of JGM of Enternational Prayerlife Institute in Phoenix, AZ. She is also a board member of the Interdenominational Services Organization of America, Inc. (ISOA). She received her communication degrees from Belmont University and Tennessee State University in Nashville, TN.

Apostle Artherrine is a Proverbs 31 woman, and was named one of "100 Outstanding Women" in Nashville, and is a recipient of the Patricia Harris Fellowship from Tennessee State University. Mother Artherrine participated as a member of the Sister Circles Steering Committee of the American Bible Society. This group participated in monthly prayer forums via conference calls with the Great Lakes Africa women leaders and trauma survivors in the Congo.

She is the devoted wife of forty-five years to Harvey Eugene Hoskins, CPA, the blessed mother of two, and a grandmother of six. They reside in Nashville, Tennessee.

"When I received the Armor of God prayer from the Power of Agreement Global Prayer Network, I felt both excited and challenged. It was another test of faith for me to follow the instructions regarding how to activate a new level of faith in my life by reciting the Armor of God prayer, commanding the day, and asking God to cover me in His precious blood daily."

— Dr. Jacqueline E. Davis
Princess Warrior, Northern Region
July 2019

Endnotes

1   Bellamy, Francis. 1971. *The Pledge of Allegiance*. Art Evans Productions.

2   Bellamy, Francis. 1971. *The Pledge of Allegiance*. Art Evans Productions.

3   Bates, Katharine Lee, 1859-1929 and Chris, Gall. 2010. "America the Beautiful".